HIS WORD in my HEART

His Word in my Heart

MEMORIZING

SCRIPTURE

FOR A CLOSER

WALK WITH GOD

Janet Pope

© 2002 by
JANET POPE

ISBN: 0-8024-1142-8

3 5 7 9 10 8 6 4

Printed in the United States of America

To Ethan,

my faithful and steadfast husband,

whose encouragement and support

made this book a reality

CONTENTS

INTRODUCTION

$\mathcal{T}$he Christian life is an odyssey, an unpredictable, arduous journey with many bends in the road and surprise encounters along the way. We are travelers in a strange place and have no control over the elements: the cold, the wind, the darkness. Uncertainty abounds, hardships are plentiful, and obstacles are inevitable. Although the struggles each of us face will vary, our destination is the same. Our Father is calling us home, and our arrival is guaranteed. The issue is not where we are going, but how we will get there.

Ten years ago, at a fork in the road, my life took the path that led me where I am today. The details are forthcoming in the early chapters of this book, but the essence of my story is that, inspired by an unknown

woman, I began to memorize long passages and entire
books of the Bible. With two small children and a
never-ending list of things to do, there were no extra
time slots in my day. I reasoned that if God wanted me
to know Him and His Word, He would make a way.
He wouldn't require something of me and then make it
impossible to achieve.

I trained myself to use moments throughout my
day to memorize Scripture when my hands were busy
but my mind was free. Household chores required
busyness but not thoughtfulness, so I included Scripture memory in my daily routines: showering, drying
my hair, folding laundry, vacuuming, waiting in traffic
or at the dentist's office. Minutes that were once idle
became opportunities to get to know God's Word.

Over the years, this practice has added up to an
enormous amount of Scripture memory, ninety-two
chapters so far. However, it is not the accomplishment
that has changed my life but the process of thinking
and meditating on specific truth learned in its context.
I saw a major difference between memorizing scattered, random verses and memorizing verses that go
together sequentially. I was not learning fragments of
truth, but whole truth, fit together the way God had
intended. I was experiencing new depth in my relationship with God as I got to know His Word one verse at a
time.

My initial motivation was strictly personal; I
wanted to get closer to God for my own well-being.
But I also knew how much influence a mother has on
her children. Without wisdom from God, where would
I lead them? God's Word, continually on my heart and
mind, brought insight and discernment to each new situation. As a mother, I wanted to teach my children the

way in which they should go, and now that role was less arbitrary.

Scripture memory became my platform as people called, asking me to share my story with the women of their church. Why? Because they too were desperate to have God and His Word as a constant source of nourishment for their weary souls. As I travel and speak across the country, I've found that women are not content to postpone a closer walk with God until they have more time. Women are hungry for God, and they need Him today for the complexities of raising a Christian family in a subtly hostile environment.

In this book I present an alternative for the frazzled, guilt-ridden woman who longs to know God and His Word but hasn't yet found a way to accomplish this amidst the unrelenting treadmill of activities. I cannot add one more hour to your day, but I can help you change the minutes and the moments you already have. My desire is to be intensely practical. Take my experience and my suggestions, and adapt them to your own situation; find what works for you.

At a recent speaking engagement in Tulsa, a woman was thanking me for my message. She said, "I've got to change my thinking habits. With all the bad news in our country, I find myself meditating on all the 'whys' and 'what-ifs,' and I am emotionally exhausted at the end of the day. I can see that my whole outlook would change if I would meditate on God's Word instead."

My intention for this book is to lead others to the oasis of God's Word. It is my hope that you will discipline your mind to trade your thoughts for God's. As you give your attention to His Word, He will meet you in unexpected places—amidst the laundry pile and the dish pile, in the car pool line and in the drive-through line. Your relationship with God will grow deeper and richer than you could ever have imagined. He will be your constant companion, your most intimate confidant.

Our pilgrimage through this life is fraught with unforeseeable hurdles, but it was never meant to be traveled alone. God gave us His Word to guide us through the lonely valleys and the immovable mountains we will face. For me, the journey has taken on new meaning. Though night is approaching, I am not afraid or hesitant to move forward. My path is illuminated, one step at a time, with His Word in my heart.

ACKNOWLEDGMENTS

I would like to recognize the following:

Melissa Treat, my treasured friend and confidant, for the hours she gave enthusiastically to read and reread every word, giving honest feedback and invaluable insight.

My weekly Precept Bible Study Group, for allowing me to take off a semester in order to finish this book. I'm thrilled to be back as your teacher and fellow learner.

Ministry Partners, who pray and give financially. Your contribution to my life and ministry is immeasurable.

1

My Story:

EVERYTHING WE NEED
FOR LIFE AND GODLINESS

The house was finally empty. All of the worldly possessions we had accumulated over eight years of marriage were meticulously stuffed into two U-Haul trucks. An uncle drove one U-Haul. Four-year-old Austin and six-year-old Natalie were eager to ride with their dad in the other for the four-hundred-mile trip, which would leave me in peaceful solitude in my own car. I relished the time alone to reflect and pray. It had been such a draining week, physically from the packing and cleaning, and emotionally from the good-byes. As we turned the corner onto the ramp of Interstate 20, I could visualize God taking us in a new direction, on a new road, to a new life. For reasons known only to God, we were moving from Dallas, Texas, to Hattiesburg, Mississippi.

Ethan and I had been in Christian ministry for thirteen years, eight years as a couple, and now God was
adding some new responsibilities to Ethan's life. God
had clearly directed our decision to move; there was no
turning back now.

After an hour of driving, I lost the Dallas Christian
radio station and was alone with my thoughts. My
mind relived memories from the last eight years: the
three houses we had remodeled while living in them
(marriage still intact), hunting for antiques in those
smothering barns in Forney, and hilarious times at Supper Club. Monumental were the joyous births of a
daughter, then a son. There was the annual Fourth of
July party with all the boiled shrimp you could peel
and, for winter fun, building the silliest-looking snow-
men in the front yard till the children's cheeks were
frozen. We wouldn't soon forget the Texas State Fair,
Bagelsteins, the Mesquite Rodeo, and of course, America's Team and *ours*, the Dallas Cowboys. Most painful
of all was leaving friends who had impacted my life.
Friends have always been important to me and good-
byes have never been easy. I was leaving my soul mate
Dawna three weeks before the birth of her second
child. Dawna had been there for me through the
mountains and the valleys, never letting me settle for
less than God's best. The blessings in our lives were too
numerous to count. There were difficult times, too,
which, in part, led to our leaving; but they were behind
us now. We would not look back.

Because of God's proven faithfulness in the past, I
knew He had a special plan for each of us. I wondered
what He had in store for me. I did not fear the future
and its uncertainties; I knew the One who held the
future, and He was going with us. I would not dwell on

the past but look expectantly to the days ahead.

We bought a seventy-year-old house we both loved, remodeled by the previous owner (yippee!) and surrounded by a yard with trees—big, tall trees. We settled in, made new friends, joined a dynamic church, and got busy with life.

A year went by, and although there was no great tragedy in our lives, I felt a growing sense of disappointment in my heart. It was not a midlife crisis; after all, I was only thirty-five. It was a crisis of unfulfilled expectations. Somehow my life was not what I had foreseen or would have chosen. I was not where I wanted to be, and I don't mean geographically. Was there something more that I was missing? Did God have a purpose for my life that was not being fulfilled? Surely this was not all God had in store for me. Scripture tells us that "hope deferred makes the heart sick" (Proverbs 13:12). I suppose that describes it best. I made known to God my frustration and inner discontent and waited for His reply.

Four new friends invited me to go with them to a Christian conference at Precept Ministries in Chattanooga, Tennessee, six hours away. If nothing else, I needed a break from the "Mom routine," and I knew I would enjoy the fellowship. It's strange to me now that I look back and see this conference as a turning point in my life. And, stranger still, it was not the content of the conference nor the friends I went with that impacted me, though both were wonderful.

What impacted my life was something that was not really part of the conference schedule at all. I was inspired by a woman from the audience who was called to the front and asked if she would share some Scripture with the group. She then quoted from memory the

entire book of Colossians. It was *awesome!* I sat there mes-
merized by what I had just heard. What would it be
like to *really know* God's Word, to have it so embedded
in your heart and mind that you could carry it with you
wherever you went? What would it mean to my relationship with God if I really knew His Word?

I had become a Christian when I was twenty-one
years old and attending the University of Florida. But
never having grown up in church, I had no Bible background or accumulated knowledge. In the years that
followed, I read through the Bible *many* times. In fact,
daily Bible reading was a discipline I held to. But I
couldn't confidently say that I *knew* the Bible. My Bible
knowledge was like a tangled pile of disconnected
wires I didn't know where or how to plug in.

I came home from Chattanooga determined to
make a change. I had come face-to-face with the shal-
lowness of my own Bible knowledge, and I knew God
was calling me into a deeper commitment to His Word.
But where would I begin? Since my inspiration had
come from someone who memorized Scripture, I
decided to follow her lead. I started with the book of
Ephesians, a challenge that without God's help would
be impossible. It took me several months, but I worked
on it every single day and night, learning one verse at a
time.

My overriding motivation was the fear of quitting.
At this point in my life, I couldn't handle the devasta-
tion of another goal abandoned. The day came when I
shared, from memory, the book of Ephesians with my
Sunday school class. As I concluded with "Grace to all
who love our Lord Jesus Christ with an undying love,"
tears began to flow and my heart pounded with joy. I
saw others with tears in their eyes, as well, but I didn't

understand what it all meant. That day, however, turned out to be a milestone in my life; the stepping-stones that preceded it were the months I spent devouring Ephesians chapter by chapter.

I couldn't say that I knew God's Word yet. What I *could* say was, "I know the book of Ephesians." And for the first time in my Christian life, I felt as though God's Word was *knowable*. I had proved that to myself. For years, I had thought that knowing the Bible was something unattainable or reserved for only a select few. But now I was convinced that the knowledge of God's Word was not beyond my reach.

At the same time, I also saw the inexhaustible nature of God's Word. Even within the book of Ephesians, after having memorized every single word, there was much more to discover. I had not yet reached the depths of its truth.

Another outcome that grew out of the many months of memorizing Ephesians was that I had a sense of *ownership* of the book. It was as though God had written it just for me. Every time I heard anything from Ephesians mentioned, in general conversation or at church, I immediately thought, *That's my book.* I had poured hours of my life into Ephesians, and now it *belonged* to me.

But why did God give me His Word, and where did He want to take me from there? I didn't know. I couldn't go back, and I couldn't stay the same; those options were no longer open to me. I wasn't sure why, or what was ahead, but I saw myself standing at a crossroads calculating a move to the right or to the left.

I was planning on teaching a Bible study in the fall on 2 Peter, so I decided that since it was several months away, I would try to memorize that Bible book. Second

Peter has only three chapters. And as I began to memorize chapter 1, saying the words out loud, over and over, implanting them into my memory, I focused on these phrases:

> Grace and peace be yours in abundance *through the knowledge of God and of Jesus our Lord.*
> ∾ 2 Peter 1:2, emphasis added

> *His divine power has given us* everything we need for life and godliness *through our knowledge of him.*
> ∾ 2 Peter 1:3, emphasis added

> *Through these he has given us his very great and precious promises, so that through them* you may participate in the divine nature.
> ∾ 2 Peter 1:4, emphasis added.

I meditated not only on the words but on the truth of what was written there. And I began to have a conversation with myself that went something like this: Wow! These are very bold statements. How could they possibly be true? This passage claims that through our knowledge of God

> ∾ we can have grace and peace in abundance,

> ∾ we can have everything we need for life and godliness,

> ∾ we can participate in the divine nature; we can become more like Jesus.

Is this *possible?* I asked. Of course, I know God's Word is true "in theory," but if it is really true that through our knowledge of Him we can have *everything* we need for life and godliness, how come more Christians aren't just pouring themselves into the Scriptures so that they can have all these things? I don't know! And I asked myself, *Well, how come* you *don't?* I sat there contemplating this challenge. Then I said, *I'm going to! I'm going to pour myself into God's Word until I get everything I need for life and godliness.*

That day, I made the right turn at the crossroads.

With renewed fervor, I plunged into God's Word as though there were no tomorrow. I was a busy mom with no more "new" hours in my day to give to this project, so I had to find ways to fit it in. But my own spiritual well-being was foundational to having the kind of family I desperately wanted, so I couldn't put it off for another day. I agonized while determining which activities were truly essential. (Can you believe my husband still thought cooking and cleaning were in the essential category?)

Over the next ten years, I memorized the Sermon on the Mount, Ephesians, Philippians, 1 Thessalonians, 2 Timothy, Titus, Hebrews, James, 1 and 2 Peter, 1 John, Revelation, as well as some of the Psalms and other passages.

In order to keep from forgetting these Scripture texts, I set up a schedule to review one book every day at the same time I was learning something new. My mind was constantly flooded with the truths of God's Word. At that time, we didn't have a Christian radio station in Hattiesburg, so instead of what I used to do in Dallas—keep the radio on all day and listen to *someone else* teach from the Bible—I worked around the house learning Scripture *for myself.* It is amazing how many things you can be doing at the same time you are learning or reviewing Scripture: showering, putting on makeup, vacuuming, folding laundry, cooking, cleaning, washing floors, driving all over town, and many other jobs that don't require thinking.

At the end of each day I was physically exhausted, but somehow I wasn't weary. In fact, I felt victorious as I constantly battled the distractions of the day and still found time for God's Word. I'm so thankful for the lessons learned that changed my attitude about God and what He requires of us. Would God want us to know Him and spend time with Him but then make it impossible to do this? No, but neither does He make it effortless. He will make a way when we demonstrate our hunger to know Him and our willingness to put Him first.

An aroma of joy began to permeate my heart and home. I wasn't the frazzled mom I used to be. The guilt caused by spiritual neglect was replaced with an urgency to make up for lost time. I had a renewed confidence that God would help me raise my children according to His plan. His presence was with me throughout my day in every decision, at every turn.

Was the desire for knowledge the sole reason for all these changes? And what did all that knowledge do for me anyway? I was aware that the Bible says, "Knowledge makes arrogant, but love edifies" (1 Corinthians 8:1 NASB), and, "If I have . . . all knowledge; . . . but do not have love, I am nothing" (1 Corinthians 13:2 NASB). Knowledge for knowledge' sake couldn't be the answer, but what about 2 Peter 1:3, "His divine power has given us everything we need for life and godliness through our knowledge of him"? The answer to this dilemma could be found in 2 Peter 1:5–8, verses that promise what knowledge can do for you.

> *For this very reason, make every effort to* add *to your* faith *goodness; and to goodness, knowledge; and to knowledge, self-control; and to self-control, perseverance; and to perseverance, godliness; and to godliness, brotherly kindness; and to brotherly kindness, love. For if you possess these qualities in increasing measure, they will keep you from being* ineffective *and* unproductive *in your* knowledge *of our Lord Jesus Christ.*
>
> ∾ 2 Peter 1:5–8, emphasis added

In other words, if you are not growing in your faith—adding to your faith—your knowledge becomes ineffective and unproductive. But, if you are continually growing in your faith, your knowledge will have a positive effect. It will keep your knowledge productive and effective. In summary, *knowledge is meaningless without application.*

People ask me, "What is the most difficult part about memorizing Scripture?" I reply, "Living it!" When I was memorizing James, I felt I was in a constant state of rebuke because there was so much in my life that needed to be changed and God was saying, "You're not living it."

James says, "Do not merely listen to the word, and so deceive yourselves. Do what it says" (James 1:22). That's telling me that if I listen to, or read, or even memorize the Word, but I don't do what it says, I'm deceived because I think I'm OK, just fine, doing well simply because I read the Word. James doesn't leave it there. He says that if you listen to the Word but don't do what it says, you're like the person who looks in the mirror, sees his flaws, but goes away forgetting to make the changes needed (James 1:23–24). In contrast is the man who looks intently into the Word, does not forget what he sees, *and makes the needed correction.* This man will be blessed in whatever he does (see v. 25). You see, the Word of God is a mirror to our souls; it reveals who we really are, inside and out.

A friend of mine, Beverly, has often worked with me, volunteering at our children's school. One day, she came to school to help out. She had been there for several hours and then went to the ladies' room. As she leaned over to wash her hands, she noticed in the mirror that she still had a curler on top of her head. She had been walking around school with that curler and no one had told her about it. But the mirror told her. Now, what do you suppose was the likelihood that after seeing the curler she left it there and walked away? None! She yanked it out immediately.

There are two important factors in this story: knowledge and application. She walked around for several hours with *no knowledge* of the problem, so how could she take action? But as soon as the mirror showed her the truth, she made the change. So it is with God's Word. Application is vital, but *we cannot apply what we do not know.*

So I saw that the two essentials must go together: knowledge and application. Knowledge is meaningless without application, and you can't have application if you don't have knowledge.

God was providing many opportunities in my own home to apply the knowledge I was learning. But it wasn't as smooth as it may have appeared from the outside looking in. The more I got into God's Word and the more knowledge I acquired, the more I felt compelled to apply it. But this became a heavy burden to me because I was exposing myself to so much. For example, when I was memorizing the Sermon on the Mount in Matthew 5–7, I could see that it was filled with humanly impossible teachings. Jesus said:

> *"But I tell you: Love your enemies and pray for those who persecute you, that you may be sons of your Father in heaven. He causes his sun to rise on the evil and the good, and sends rain on the righteous and the unrighteous. If you love those who love you, what reward will you get? Are not even the tax collectors doing that? And if you greet only your brothers, what are you doing more than others? Do not even pagans do that?"*
>
> ∽ Matthew 5:44–47

Such powerful words and a call to a lifestyle so far from my own! I was having trouble loving my friends, and now I'm supposed to love my enemies?

Why did God give me His Word if it only points out my inadequacies and failure to live up to its principles? My own knowledge was overwhelming me! My constant prayer was, "Lord, I want to go *beyond* knowledge. I don't want to be one of those people who can quote the Bible but whose life is a disgrace to the cause of Christ. O God, I'd rather *die* than be that person."

The Lord knew the quandary I was in, but He had already shown me the answer. It was in the book of Ephesians—had I forgotten so quickly the meaning of those words? This is Paul's prayer for the Ephesians; notice the word *power* throughout.

*For this reason I kneel before the Father, from whom his
whole family in heaven and on earth derives its name. I
pray that out of his glorious riches he may strengthen you
with* power *through his Spirit in your inner being, so that
Christ may dwell in your hearts through faith. And I pray
that you, being rooted and established in love, may have*
power, *together with all the saints, to grasp how wide and
long and high and deep is the love of Christ, and to know
this love that* surpasses knowledge—*that you may be
filled to the measure of all the fullness of God.*

*Now to him who is able to do immeasurably more than all
we ask or imagine, according to* his power that is at
work within us, *to him be glory in the church and in
Christ Jesus throughout all generations, for ever and ever!
Amen.*

∽ Ephesians 3:14–21, emphasis added

It is God who gives me the power to know the
depth and breadth of His love; and it is only knowing
the love of Christ that will surpass knowledge. God
was showing me that on my own I am incapable of living up to His Word. It will only be God's power working in me and through me that will enable me to go
beyond knowledge.

God was leading me step-by-step in my understanding, teaching me what it meant to really know
Him and walk with Him. I had tasted knowledge, and
it was delightfully satisfying. But I had also become
intensely aware of my own indigence, my desperate
need for His presence in order to make knowledge
more than just words on a page. I see now that God
had me right where He wanted me. He was just beginning to write His Word in my heart.

My Goal:

LIKE A TREE PLANTED BY STREAMS OF WATER

During my teenage years, my family lived on a lake in Winter Park, Florida. In the backyard, we had a cypress tree that lived right at the water's edge. It was a favorite place to sit and talk, or just rest, watching the waves splash up against the tree. Even in the scorching Florida sun, that tree was never parched; the water was its life source. In contrast to that, we had a huge oak tree in the front yard that was blanketed with thick Spanish moss. It was a grand, stately tree, but every year it lost more and more branches because of the impact of the moss taking over. This is a vivid picture to me of two contrasting lives: one that is thriving, one that is withering. What will be the deciding factor as to which tree my life resembles? It will be whatever I allow as the dominant influence in my life.

Psalm 1 describes a man who is compared to a tree. These are the first three verses:

> *Blessed is the man*
> *who does not walk in the counsel of the wicked*
> *or stand in the way of sinners*
> *or sit in the seat of mockers.*
> *But his delight is in the law of the* LORD,
> *and on his law he meditates day and night.*
> *He is like a tree planted by streams of water,*
> *which yields its fruit in season*
> *and whose leaf does not wither.*
> *Whatever he does prospers.*
> ∾ Psalm 1:1–3

What kind of person does God call *blessed?* One whose life is not swayed by ungodly men and who is influenced by meditating day and night on God's Word. How does God describe that person? He is "like a tree planted by streams of water," continually nourished, never thirsty. This man will yield fruit in season, when God's time is right. Because his mind and heart delight in God's Word, his actions will be God-centered and divinely prosperous.

In the previous chapter, I told you how the writings of the apostle Peter had challenged my thinking by asserting that God had given me everything I needed for life and godliness *through* my knowledge of Him. Grace and peace would be mine in abundance *through* my knowledge of Him. God gave us His Word so that we might *know* Him. Could this be why the psalmist decreed a blessing on the man who would meditate on God's law day and night? The connection is both obvious and profound. The man who meditates on God's Word day and night will have an increasing knowledge of God, and in knowing Him, he will have everything he needs for life and godliness. He will be watered and nourished, bearing fruit in season and prospering in all he does. No wonder he is called blessed. There is no higher attainment for any child of God.

The first few years I was memorizing Scripture, I was very enthusiastic about it and wondered why every Christian didn't memorize Scripture. Maybe God didn't want everyone to; maybe it was optional. I began to investigate. I went to the Bible first. Was there a command to memorize Scripture? I couldn't locate one. I couldn't even find the word *memorize*. I searched even the Greek and the Hebrew and couldn't find a word that meant "to memorize." Do I hear a sigh of relief out there? No, the Bible does *not* command us to memorize Scripture. But here are some of the commands and exhortations we do find:

∾ Know God's Word.

∾ Remember His Word.

∾ Do not forget His commandments.

∾ Have His Word ready on our lips.

∾ Meditate on His law day and night.

∾ Dwell on Christ's words.

∾ Store up His words.

∾ Keep God's Word within our hearts.

For me, memorizing Scripture is just a vehicle for accomplishing those objectives. God desires for us to know Him intimately, and that's why He gave us His written Word. It is God's revelation of Himself. He left nothing out that He wants us to know. There are many avenues that lead us into a greater knowledge of His Word, and memorizing is just one of them.

The goal is to know God and to walk closely with Him—nothing more, nothing less.

A friend told me recently that her mother was berating her because her children didn't know the Lord's Prayer. They had not memorized it. She told her mother, "But they know *how* to pray, and they *do* pray." That wasn't good enough for her mother. She wanted it memorized! Had she missed the point of the Lord's Prayer herself? It was never intended to be a memorized prayer. Its purpose was to teach the disciples to pray. Memorizing is never the final goal; it is only a tool to help us reach the ultimate goal of knowing God and loving Him.

Consider these words of Moses. "Fix these words of mine in your hearts and minds; tie them as symbols on your hands and bind them on your foreheads" (Deuteronomy 11:18). Moses was saying, in effect, "Make sure God's words are written on your heart and your mind. Impress them into the very core of your life. Make them as permanent as possible."

The reference to binding words to the hands and forehead can be interpreted symbolically as all of your actions (your hands) and all of your thoughts (your forehead). God's Word is to be central in all that we are, all that we do, and all that we think about. It is so important, so vital to our character and our behavior, that we must *do whatever it takes* to keep God foremost in our lives. That can mean reading God's Word, listening to God's Word, studying God's Word, teaching God's Word, meditating and thinking about God's Word, and memorizing God's Word.

I know many godly men and women who study and revere God's Word but do not memorize it. They have no doubt found other ways of keeping His Word at the center of their lives. In my own life, however, profound changes came about when I began to memorize Scripture, and I can no longer keep silent about the impact it can have.

If God is directing us to meditate on His Word day and night, what exactly does it mean to meditate? Our common understanding of meditation is to think deeply about something, to ponder, to contemplate.

However, an accurate understanding of the biblical term requires digging into the Old Testament. The Hebrew transliteration of the term is *haghah*. The literal meaning of this term is "to murmur; to mutter; to growl; to sigh; to moan; to roar; to meditate; to muse; to speak; to whisper."[1] Did you notice that many of these terms involve making sounds with your mouth, speaking words quietly to yourself? This new insight reveals to us that our biblical instruction is to go beyond just *thinking* about God's Word, but is to extend to *actually saying the words out loud*. The Septuagint (Greek translation of the Old Testament) compares the meaning to that of rehearsing a speech before you give it.[2] This definition implies that the purpose is not for anyone but the one doing the meditating.

A conventional teaching technique employed universally is to combine seeing, hearing, and speaking to augment the learning process. These three are also used in meditation. As we see and say and hear the words over and over, we are allowing the transforming power of God's Word to alter our thinking, our behavior, and our very lives.

In the twenty references on meditation given in the Psalms, what was the psalmist meditating on? God's Word, God's work, God's ways, God's wonders. Those were the things the Israelites rehearsed with their minds and their lips. In referring to Old Testament meditation, G. B. Funderburk tells us, "It is a most rewarding act of worship, of spiritual renewal, of mental refreshing, and of divine communion."[3] That is what I have found to be true in my own experience of memorizing Scripture. It has become an act of worship, ushering me into God's throne room and keeping me spiritually renewed each day. As a busy wife and mother, with an entire household affected by my demeanor, I cannot afford to miss a single day of fellowship with God; the consequences are too far-reaching.

In many of the religions that have permeated our society, meditation involves *emptying* your mind for the purpose of relaxation, detoxifying your body and soul, and relieving stress. In contrast, the biblical concept of meditation is to *fill* your mind with God's thoughts and character and purposes. There is no greater relief from stress than to know that I am abiding in God's presence, free from bondage to myself and to the world's philosophies.

If you have had good results from meditating on Scripture *without* memorizing it, you are a rare breed, the exception to the norm. For most of us, the problem with meditating is that we begin with a great thought and two minutes later we're thinking about our list of things to do, our errands, and the phone calls we need to make. We are easily distracted because our minds get lost without something specific to focus on. This is where memorizing Scripture is so helpful. You have a specific focus, a specific thought, specific words.

Let's say, for example, that you are going to memorize Psalm 103 during a one-month period. You begin on the morning of day one, with verse 1, "Praise the LORD, O my soul; all my inmost being, praise his holy name." Throughout the day, this one verse is your focus. You say it out loud over and over. You think about each word and its meaning. You let your mind dwell on it. You absorb it into your heart. This is meditation.

The next day, you add verse 2, "Praise the LORD, O my soul, and forget not all his benefits." As you say these two verses throughout your day, you are instilling into your heart the importance of not forgetting all His benefits. You can't wait for the next few days to get into the list of these benefits:

> *who forgives all your sins*
> *and heals all your diseases,*
> *who redeems your life from the pit*
> *and crowns you with love and compassion,*
> *who satisfies your desires with good things*
> *so that your youth is renewed like the eagle's.*
> ∽ *Psalm 103:3–5*

By the time you have finished the psalm, you will have spent an entire month meditating on God's immeasurable love for you. You will be acutely aware of His presence in your daily experience, and your heart will overflow with praise and gratefulness. Like a cup running over, you will not be able to contain your joy that the God of the universe would choose to love you so much. You will also have accomplished both the goal of meditation and the goal of memorizing Scripture.

The influence of God's Word will affect a multitude of areas that need overhauling. A notable change in me was my sporadic prayer life. In years past, prayer had been an obligation but not a pleasure. I knew I was supposed to pray without ceasing, pray about everything, and pray for others. But I got bogged down with myriad requests on behalf of dozens of people, and I had no idea how to intercede for them. My prayer journal had page after page of what I considered to be unanswered prayers. But who was I to say that God didn't answer their prayers? He probably said no with good reason. I felt as though I was trying to manipulate God or force His hand, even though I had no clue what was best for these people. Yet I felt guilty and selfish if I didn't pray for those who had asked me to.

Every few weeks, I crumpled up my prayer list, threw it away, and started over. Probably what concerned me the most was that I didn't want to waste time on meaningless prayers and forget the really important things. But what *were* the important things? Prayer had become one of those onerous chores. It was an acknowledged duty but one I didn't enjoy. And quite frankly, I wasn't convinced that my prayers made much difference. You could say I had a warped view of prayer. Or was it just an unbiblical one?

The more I spent time in God's Word, the more my perspective opened up. My prayers were gaining fresh momentum with revitalized objectives. The goal in prayer is not to convince God to do what *I* want but to bring my desires in alignment with what *He* wants. So what is it that He wants? We can only know this as we come to know His Word and thus know His desires. *God's glory and God's honor and the fulfillment of His kingdom* are to be the focus of our prayers. That's the way Jesus prayed. He had no ulterior motives.

Let's say, for example, that a friend asks for prayer regarding a difficult situation she finds herself in. I don't know God's direction in this, but I do know some specific things from my study and memorization of the Scriptures that can be applied. I know it is God's will that in the midst of her circumstances she keep seeking God with all her heart and walk in surrender to Him. I know it is God's will that He be honored, that His purposes be fulfilled in her life, and that Christ be seen in her character. I don't have to try to figure out God's plan. I know the Holy Spirit is interceding for me in the perfect will of God. This has given me a great deal of confidence in prayer.

I pray for my husband and children the things I know are true in Scripture. I pray that they would walk in integrity, manifesting God's attributes; that they would live as worthy representatives of God's kingdom; and that God would bring to completion the work He has begun in them. These are all prayers that reflect God's will.

In our prayer room at church, there are dozens of requests for health-related problems. It's not necessary for me to know God's sovereign will. I pray something for each one for which I have absolute certainty:

    ∿ That God would use their infirmity to draw them closer to Him

    ∿ That they would learn steadfastness in suffering

∾ That others would see Christ in them and so want to know Him

∾ That, whatever the outcome, God would be honored and His kingdom furthered

There is enormous power in these kinds of prayers. And how much better to pray in this way than to pray simply for a healing, if their lives are not changed in the process.

As I review Scripture throughout the day, God may bring someone to mind I should pray for with a specific verse. Wow, what a privilege! James tells us, "The prayer of a righteous man is powerful and effective" (James 5:16). I've come a long way, and the journey is just beginning. The aim of a meaningful prayer life is to keep in touch with God and walk in close communion with Him.

A healthy relationship with God requires a two-way interchange. He communicates with me through His Word, and I speak to Him through prayer. Where my skills have been lacking, He has taught me how to reach His heart. It's OK to pray about material things, but we must not lose sight of God's purposes on a grander scale. That is what Scripture has done for me. My prayers have a new direction, new content, and, best of all, a new outcome.

What you will see in this book is that I am advocating memorizing passages and books instead of random, scattered verses. It is my personal opinion that memorizing passages, chapters, or entire books is more beneficial than memorizing seventy-five independent verses. If one of your goals is to grow in your understanding of God, then you will get a more complete picture if you memorize verses that go together. For example, the book of Philippians was God's complete message to the church at Philippi, and the book of Ephesians was God's complete message to the church at Ephesus. Memorizing entire books or passages will keep intact God's succession of ideas, without interruption.

Many individual verses, memorized out of context, can give a false meaning. Would you be surprised to know that one verse, John 3:16, has given many people a false assurance of their salvation? How could this be? Because they don't know the context in which the verse is found. If they knew John 3 in its entirety, they would know that

∞ you must be born again (vv. 3–7);

∞ those who know and believe the truth will have deeds that prove their belief (vv. 19–21); and

∞ those who believe have eternal life; but those who do not obey the Son of God shall not see life but God's wrath abides on them (v. 36).

By memorizing verses 1–21 instead of verse 16 by itself, you will avoid a misinterpretation because you will get the entire conversation between Jesus and Nicodemus. There are many examples of verses that need supporting verses to get an accurate interpretation of them. By memorizing verses that go together, you will avoid wrong thinking that leads to wrong application.

Have you ever noticed that individual verses we

choose to memorize are often self-focused? We're looking for what we can get from God. For example,

> *Delight yourself in the Lord; and He will* give you the
> desires of your heart.
> ∞ Psalm 37:4 NASB, emphasis added

> *And my God will* supply all your needs *according to
> His riches in glory in Christ Jesus.*
> ∞ Philippians 4:19 NASB, emphasis added

> No good thing does He withhold *from those who
> walk uprightly.*
> ∞ Psalm 84:11 NASB, emphasis added

> *He who did not spare His own Son, but delivered Him over
> for us all, how will He not also with Him* freely give us
> all things?
> ∞ Romans 8:32 NASB, emphasis added

I had memorized each one of these verses years ago
as a new Christian, so that I could be sure God would
give me everything I needed and wanted. The focus
was definitely on me. I'm not saying we shouldn't memorize these verses, but if we will memorize them in
their context, we will keep the focus on God and
greatly enhance our learning in the process. God put
His thoughts and His words in a particular order within
each book, and this is how God intended for us to learn
them.

The challenge of memorizing large portions—
whole chapters or entire books—seems to intimidate

people. They think it will be more difficult or time-consuming than memorizing random, individual verses. I don't believe that is true. Let me tell you about a man in my church. He told me that his goal for the year was to memorize Philippians. There are 104 verses in the book and fifty-two weeks in a year. This equates to memorizing two verses a week. Does this sound difficult or time-consuming to you?

If he accomplishes his goal—and I hope he will—he'll be motivated next year to take on another book. There are many books with fewer verses than Philippians, which means that at the same pace of two verses per week, he could have *ten books memorized in ten years*. That doesn't seem possible, but it is. Well, now you know that I wasn't working as hard as you thought I was! Just a few verses a week adds up to a lot.

By far, the keystone in memorizing is reviewing. This is why passages are much simpler, because you can review an entire chapter, about twenty-one verses, in less than three minutes, without stopping to name the references. It also gives you God's unified flow of thought as His Word unfolds.

The biggest surprise when I tell people about my Scripture memory is the time factor. Contrary to what most people think, it takes very little time to memorize Scripture, because you can do it while you do other things. Because of the value of God's Word in my life, I don't want to go even one day without spending time in the Word. But a goal of studying God's Word every single day is unrealistic for me. I suppose if I had no husband, no children, no job, and lived in a full-service hotel, I could manage to study God's Word every day. But my life is jam-packed, and I know yours is also. There have been days when I have been so busy serv-

ing the Lord and my family that I have fallen into bed
exhausted and have not even opened my Bible all day.
But, thanks to memorizing Scripture, it is a very rare
day when I have not spent time in God's Word. That is
because I have made it the habit of my life to memorize
and review Scripture throughout the day.

Many people ask me if it's my goal to memorize the
whole Bible. I tell them no. This answer isn't what
they're expecting. Honestly, I have no aspirations of
becoming a Bible trivia queen or even the Bible answer
woman. I want God's Word to be written on my heart
so that my life reflects that I'm a woman who knows
God and walks closely with Him.

It is not my goal in life to look back and count my
accomplishments. It is not to build a reputation or to
receive earthly acclaim. I know that I will have lived
well if I can say that God has been my absolute delight
and my companion throughout my days and that His
Word has been a steady flow of water for my thirsty
soul. I will be truly blessed beyond measure if I can be
counted with the man in Psalm 1.

3
Your Turn:
ON HIS LAW HE MEDITATES DAY AND NIGHT

Today we're going to try an experiment. It's your turn to see what memorizing God's Word can do for you. I always recommend that you start out with something very small, so that you will get a taste but nothing overwhelming. Psalm 1 is a perfect place to start. It is short, only six verses, but more important, its message gives you the motivation to memorize God's Word. It tells you what the benefits will be of meditating on God's Word day and night.

If you already know Psalm 1 by heart, let me suggest Psalm 121. It is eight verses long, and its theme is *God watching over us.* Other options might be Psalm 4; Psalm 8; Psalm 23; or Psalm 100.

People often ask me if I have a great method for

memorizing Scripture. I tell them, "No, but I have great motivation. If you are highly motivated, any method will do." I'm going to share my plain and simple method and get you started, so that this little exercise will inspire you to continue.

You will want to pick a version of the Bible that you like best. It will be easier if you choose the one you are most familiar with. I always memorize in the *New International Version*, but I study and teach from the *New American Standard Bible*. This gets confusing sometimes, but it has also helped me understand certain passages. It will be less complicated if you stick with the Scripture version you know best. I do not recommend paraphrases. They are not accurate translations but rather someone's opinion. If you're going to put some effort into this, you may as well get the genuine article. Don't forget that inherent in God's Word is the power to transform your life. That's why we are doing this.

The first thing I do is to write out what I want to memorize on the 3 x 5 index cards that are held together on a spiral. Stores sell packets containing fifty index cards attached with a spiral wire so you won't have separate cards scattered all over your house and car. I buy these at the grocery store, but any office supply will also have them. A set of 4 x 6 cards will work just as well, but they take up too much room in my purse. An alternative is to copy that page out of your Bible. What you want is something you can take with you easily. It can be cumbersome to carry your Bible around everywhere.

When you write out your verses, put the reference number at the far left so that you can keep track of where you are. (I put the verse number only, with a colon just before it to remind me this is a verse number and not a chapter number.) We will not be memorizing the numbers because they are not important and can be distracting from the message.

Do not lose sight of your goal. It's not the memorization itself that is important but the constant reflection on God, His character, and His ways. The psalmist writes, "Seven times a day I praise you for your righteous laws" (Psalm 119:164). The number *seven* is not suggesting an exact number but rather a continual turning to God's Word throughout the day. With this in mind, you're ready to begin.

Day One

:1 BLESSED IS THE MAN
WHO DOES NOT WALK IN THE COUNSEL OF THE WICKED
OR STAND IN THE WAY OF SINNERS
OR SIT IN THE SEAT OF MOCKERS.

∾ I like to begin first thing in the morning, but let's not wait.

∾ Go ahead and try this one verse. Take it phrase by phrase, line by line. See how far you can get.

∾ Concentrate on the verse. Say it out loud, over and over.

∾ How many times today can you review this verse? *At least a dozen times.*

∾ It takes less than ten seconds to say this one verse. You can fit that in just about anywhere.

∽ Take your index spiral with you wherever you go: into the kitchen, driving in your car.

∽ Review while you hang up clothes in the laundry room or while you wait at school in the carpool line.

∽ Ask, "Who is God calling blessed?" This psalm begins by saying what the blessed man does *not* do. Come back to this verse throughout your day, during lunch, at the water fountain.

∽ Focus on what is being said. Evaluate your own life. Does this describe you?

∽ Take the last few minutes of your day to review and reflect.

∽ Ask God to give you discipline and an expectant heart as you learn these verses.

Day Two

:2 BUT HIS DELIGHT IS IN THE LAW OF THE LORD,
AND ON HIS LAW HE MEDITATES DAY AND NIGHT.

∽ Begin reviewing verse 1 first thing in the morning. Say it in the shower.

∽ See if you can remember the verse without looking.

∽ Move on to verse 2. Say them both together. Repeat the two verses out loud.

℞ Now you're up to about fifteen seconds. I told you it doesn't take a lot of time.

℞ The psalm now tells us what the blessed man does.

℞ Think about the verse and the man. Notice the contrast between verses 1 and 2.

℞ What does it mean to delight in God's law? Does this verse describe you? Do you want it to?

℞ Take your index spiral with you everywhere.

℞ Sit it on the counter when you're making breakfast, coffee, and school lunches.

℞ Review while you drive in your car, while you're waiting at your hair appointment, or while you're waiting in the dentist's office.

℞ Turn the radio off and let your mind dwell on these truths.

℞ Before you go to bed, sit still, review your verses, and make them a prayer to God.

Day Three

:3 HE IS LIKE A TREE PLANTED BY STREAMS OF WATER,
WHICH YIELDS ITS FRUIT IN SEASON
AND WHOSE LEAF DOES NOT WITHER.
WHATEVER HE DOES PROSPERS.

℞ Start your day by reviewing your first two verses.

∽ If you reviewed the verses fifteen or twenty times yesterday, then they should come right back to you.

∽ Your biggest block of time is probably while getting dressed. It takes me at least thirty minutes to shower, dry my hair, and put on makeup and clothes.

∽ Begin your new verse while you are getting ready. Say it phrase by phrase, line by line, moving slowly.

∽ Share the verse with your spouse, or with your kids, or with the mirror. It all works.

∽ Think about today's verse. How is the man described? What characterizes his life?

∽ How is it possible that whatever he does prospers? Does this happen overnight or does it take time?

∽ You are now up to about twenty-five seconds of review time. What a great way to spend twenty-five seconds!

∽ Take the verses with you throughout your day, and fit in lots of review whenever you can.

∽ Household chores are not so laborious when you add Scripture: vacuuming, unloading the dishwasher, folding laundry, sweeping the front porch, even taking the garbage to the alley (not one of my chores).

∽ Before you go to bed, sit still, clear your mind, and review your verses.

✍ Surrender your heart and life afresh to God. Ask Him to write these words on your heart.

Day Four

:4 NOT SO THE WICKED!
THEY ARE LIKE CHAFF THAT THE WIND BLOWS AWAY.

✍ As soon as you wake up, begin reviewing your first three verses.

✍ Then add today's verse. Review them all together. You'll be up to thirty seconds review time.

✍ Say these verses ten or more times while getting ready for your day.

✍ Think about the new verse. Say it out loud, over and over.

✍ What is "not so" about the wicked? *They do not prosper.*

✍ Why not? *Because they are like chaff that the wind blows away.*

✍ What is chaff? *It's the useless part of the grain that comes off during threshing.*

✍ Take your verses with you and practice them while you run errands.

✍ Look over the verses while you're waiting at the bank drive-through, piano lessons, soccer practice, and the copy machine. A lot of precious time can be redeemed while waiting.

✎ Recite your verses to a friend. Ask your friend to check on your progress next week.

✎ Before going to bed, review a few times. Trust God to make these words a reality in your life.

Day Five

:5 THEREFORE THE WICKED WILL NOT STAND IN THE JUDGMENT,
NOR SINNERS IN THE ASSEMBLY OF THE RIGHTEOUS.

✎ When the alarm clock sounds, begin reviewing your verses. You've got the hang of it now.

✎ Add verse 5 and review them all together. You're at about thirty-five seconds now.

✎ Say the verses out loud, over and over.

✎ Repeat your verses while fixing breakfast and throwing clothes in the laundry.

✎ Share the verses with your spouse and kids, even the cat.

✎ Review while you drive to work or to school. Turn off the radio for a few minutes so that you can think.

✎ Meditate on what today's verse means. It is a conclusion, a summary statement.

✎ There is a day of reckoning coming. You will want to be one who is standing.

❧ Come back to your verses at lunch or during a work break.

❧ Let God speak this truth to your heart. Drink in these words.

❧ Review while cooking dinner and doing the dishes.

❧ Take a reflective moment before bedtime and think of the joy you have brought to the Father today.

Day Six

:6 FOR THE LORD WATCHES OVER THE WAY OF THE
   RIGHTEOUS,
BUT THE WAY OF THE WICKED WILL PERISH.

❧ Give your first thoughts of the day to review your five verses. Can you do it without looking?

❧ Keep your verses on the counter where you are doing your hair and makeup.

❧ Add today's verse. Say it out loud over and over and over. Concentrate.

❧ Keep reviewing while you iron your clothes for the day and while you make the beds.

❧ The forty seconds for this psalm are time well spent.

❧ Think about this final verse. The Lord is watching over you. What a comforting thought.

∞ Ask yourself the hard questions. Does this psalm call for a change in my life?

∞ Do you long to be the one who God calls blessed? Now you know how. Go after it.

∞ Don't be discouraged; you are already on your way. Ask God to help you develop good habits.

∞ Train your mind to run to God's Word, day-dreaming with His thoughts.

∞ Practice these verses throughout your day, whenever you can squeeze in forty seconds.

∞ Rehearse the words while feeding your animals or picking up around the house or yard.

∞ Save the last few minutes of your day to thank God for His words of life.

∞ Go to sleep while thinking and praying about the transformation God has for you.

Day Seven

∞ Start the day by reviewing all of Psalm 1. Go over it several times, out loud.

∞ Thank God for His faithfulness in helping you absorb His Word.

∞ Carry your verses throughout the house, into your car, and everywhere you go.

∞ Call a friend and bless her day with these verses.

∞ You have been meditating on God's Word day and night for seven days. How does it feel?

∞ Relish in the joy of a goal accomplished. Congratulate yourself. Your Father is well pleased.

∞ Ask God to stir in your heart a longing for more truth.

∞ Keep reviewing throughout your day, while you are jogging, exercising, or walking the dog.

∞ Repeat the words again around dinnertime.

∞ Make your final review before bed, taking time to reflect on your journey this week.

∞ Determine in your soul to stay in God's Word and truly make His Word your delight.

Look back over the last seven days and evaluate. What are you most encouraged by? How is your outlook on life? Have you found more free moments than you thought you had? Are there more to be captured? Do you feel nourished and sustained? Is your soul strengthened and fortified? Is God true to His Word? Yes, always. Keep going, my friend; there is more.

Now that you have Psalm 1 firmly fixed in your mind, how will you make sure that you will not forget these verses you have worked so diligently to remember? Here is my advice. Pick a certain day of the week on which you will review Psalm 1—for example, Mondays. This will be the day you always review Psalm 1, no matter what else you go on to memorize. Remember, it will only take forty seconds to do this. If you don't have it memorized flawlessly, spend some more time working on it. At the end of a year, you will have reviewed the psalm at least fifty-two times. This process will move it from short-term memory to long-term memory, so that you will never, ever forget it.

When I am speaking to a group, I like to ask, "How many of you know the Pledge of Allegiance to the flag, by memory?" Virtually all of those who grew up in the United States will raise their hands. "How did you accomplish that? Because you said it five days a week for twelve years. Will you ever forget it? No, because it's stored in your long-term memory." This same principle applies to Scripture memory. You move information from short-term memory to long-term memory by repetition. That's why reviewing is so important.

For many of you, the pace of one verse a day has been too slow. You are hungry and eager to tackle more verses in a shorter period of time. Don't let me hold you back. Do as much as you are comfortable with. Your goal should be to find the pace that keeps you meditating on God's Word all day long. I recommend at least one verse a day in order to discipline your mind. For example, if you only attempt one verse per week, that does not force you to keep bringing your thoughts back to God throughout your day. When I first began memorizing, I took on more verses in a week's time than I do presently. And yet the total time spent meditating is probably about the same. It's just that now I'm devoting a significant part of each day to reviewing my other books.

In chapter 5, I am going to give you a bigger challenge, now that you have conquered Psalm 1. Don't be intimidated. Longer passages are not more difficult. You learn them exactly the same way. Some people think I must have a photographic memory. This is not true! My two teenagers would love to tell you that I am *not* the sharpest pencil in the drawer. When it comes to helping with homework, I cannot remember any history, any geometry, any science, or any other subject. I would not get far on *Who Wants to Be a Millionaire?* So why have I been so successful at memorizing Scripture? It's because I have a higher goal than just to memorize the Bible. My goal is to know God and walk closely with Him. This is why I've made it the habit of my life, a daily discipline.

I received the following e-mail several months after a speaking engagement:

> Hi Janet! I have been wanting to let you know how your words have borne fruit in my life. I am very reluctant to jump into people's "programs," as I often experience more frustration than progress, so I really only went to your seminar because my friend Renée wanted to attend! (True confessions) And to underscore that, I really only began to memorize the Scripture because Renée said, "Let's both do Psalm 119!"
>
> I enjoyed what you shared and agreed that Scripture memory is important, but it was hearing you recite it that made me want to do it, because it was then that I knew the Scripture was not just in your head but in your heart. However, I still needed Renée's push to get started.
>
> Anyway, I have been wanting to let you know that simply doing a verse a day and doing whole portions of Scripture have been wonderfully used in my life. A couple of years ago I began weight lifting and experienced lots of physical benefits, and I compare what is happening in my mind and heart to that. It's sort of like taking vitamins for my soul. Anyway, I wanted to encourage you,

as this has been the most significant "power surge" I
have experienced since I first became a believer!

In Christ, Karen.

That e-mail was a great boost for me, and that's
why I'm sharing it. You may also need a little push. If
so, let Karen's words be your incentive.
Let me share with you one more brief passage that
gives the rationale for memorizing Scripture.

How can a young man keep his way pure?
By living according to your word.
I seek you with all my heart;
do not let me stray from your commands.
I have hidden your word in my heart
that I might not sin against you.
Praise be to you, O LORD;
teach me your decrees.
With my lips I recount
all the laws that come from your mouth.
I rejoice in following your statutes
as one rejoices in great riches.
I meditate on your precepts
and consider your ways.
I delight in your decrees;
I will not neglect your word.
➷ Psalm 119:9–16, emphasis added

Do you suppose this author was in the habit of memorizing God's Word? I would think so. Clearly he made God's Word an indispensable part of his life. We don't know who wrote this longest psalm, but his purpose is clear, to extol the virtues of God's Word and to point us in that same direction.

> *I lift up my hands to your commands, which I love,*
> *and I meditate on your decrees.*
> ∞ Psalm 119:48

4

Benefit #1:

KNOWLEDGE WILL BE PLEASANT TO YOUR SOUL

The story is told of Martin Luther, a priest in the six-teenth century whose entire theology and mission in life were altered when he fully grasped the meaning of Romans 1:17, "The just shall live by faith" (KJV). On the basis of that single verse, he led the Protestant Reformation and pointed the world to salvation by grace, through faith, and not by works. Can one verse of Scripture change the course of a person's life? Yes, if he purposes in his heart to believe it. Such was the case for me with this verse: "His divine power has given us everything we need for life and godliness through our knowledge of him" (2 Peter 1:3).

I have only begun to tell you the profound impression this one verse has made on my approach to life and the direction I have taken. When I made that conscious decision, choosing to take God at His Word, I was compelled to travel on a different route. I changed my focus, deliberately pursuing the knowledge of God, with no reserve and no Plan B. If this declaration from God, "Everything we need for life and godliness," was true, then it was surely the most fantastic promise in the Bible, and I wasn't going to miss out on it. Though I have no plans of starting any Reformation, I am nonetheless burdened to convince the Christian world of the significance of this one verse.

As I gave careful attention to the Word, my knowledge of God was compounding daily. I was truly amazed at all I was learning. But did I get everything I needed for life and godliness? Strangely enough, as the months and years went by, I never stopped to wonder what those things were. I just knew that He would provide them. Looking back, I am in awe when I see that God began with my greatest need!

As a child of God, my most indispensable need is to have a meaningful, adoring relationship with the One I call Lord and Father. My soul would be impoverished without the opportunity to commune with God, relating to Him as a child with her Daddy, or a devoted servant with a loving Master. This is what I have found through His Word, increasing joy in His companionship and a gratified heart that seeks no other source. His Word continually ushers me into His presence and feeds me at His table. This has been, by far, the greatest benefit of knowing God's Word. If to know Him is to love Him, then to know Him greatly is to love Him greatly.

Why should I find it so astounding that my greatest need was His greatest command? His preeminent requirement of me was the thing I needed most. You remember when Jesus was asked, "Which is the quintessential commandment?" He answered, "Love the Lord your God with all your heart and with all your soul and with all your mind and with all your strength" (Mark 12:28–30). God's utmost desire for you and for me is that we love Him. And what we need most for life and godliness is an abiding relationship with God.

By the very inclusion of the word *all*—all your heart, all your soul, all your mind, and all your strength—it is clear that Jesus was specifying a progressive love, one that involves more and more, not less and less, until every aspect of our being belongs to Him. God is asking a lot of us. Why is that? Because the totality of our life flows from that relationship. Everything we attempt to do in serving God and serving others is the result of the preeminence God has in our lives.

But how can we fulfill this supreme command to love God if we do not know the object of our affection? How can we love God if we don't know Him? And what about the intensity of love demanded? If our knowledge of God is shallow, how can our love be deep?

This is where I had been short-circuiting my relationship with God. By not going deeper into His Word, I was not accelerating my knowledge of God; and consequently my love for God was less than it could be. I didn't love God more because I wasn't getting to know God more.

As I devoted myself to pursuing the knowledge of God, my heart was being drawn to His. The apostle John tells us that "we love [God] because he first loved us" (1 John 4:19). This is true. Our love for God is in response to His abundant love for us. He was and is the initiator of our relationship. Now I can see why Paul prayed that we would *know* the depth and breadth of the love of God, for only then can we *love* Him in return. I don't think it was ever registered in my brain that my *love for God* would depend on my *knowledge of His love for me.* But sure enough, the more I knew Him, the more I loved Him. How simple it all seems now, so elementary, to say that my greatest need for life and godliness was to love God more.

Luke records in his Gospel the story of the time Simon the Pharisee asked Jesus to dine at his home. While Jesus was reclining at the table, an immoral woman from the city came in. She began to weep, wetting Jesus' feet with her tears and wiping them with her hair. Simon was indignant, thinking that Jesus should know what kind of woman she was and thus shun her.

> *Jesus answered him, "Simon, I have something to tell you."*
>
> *"Tell me, teacher," he said.*
>
> *"Two men owed money to a certain moneylender. One owed him five hundred denarii, and the other fifty. Neither of them had the money to pay him back, so he canceled the debts of both. Now which of them will love him more?"*
>
> *Simon replied, "I suppose the one who had the bigger debt canceled."*
>
> *"You have judged correctly," Jesus said.*
>
> ∽ Luke 7:40–43

Where I see myself in this story is not that I have sinned more or less than anybody else but that I have realized through His Word the depth of my sin, God's abhorrence of sin, and what it cost Jesus to release me from it.

Ten years ago, I might have compared my sins to the man who owed fifty denarii. Now I better understand the gravity of sin and all that sin encompasses, so I see myself more as the man who owed five hundred denarii. And I am more grateful and more appreciative, and there is no doubt that this knowledge has made me love Him more.

In terms of human relationships, one might easily conclude that if you want to love someone more you must (1) get to know them and (2) be their friend. That doesn't sound complicated, but what we often overlook in our relationship with God is that we must come to Him on His terms, not ours. For example, we could brainstorm, asking all the ways we could get to know God. However, a more appropriate question is "How did *God* plan for us to know Him?" That's the issue. It's not how we are planning to get to know God, but how *God* intended for us to know Him. The answer is that *He gave us His written Word.* This was His plan. The Holy Scriptures are God's complete revealed message to His beloved children. He gave us the Bible so that we could know Him.

Then why are we looking in so many other places? On occasion, I have heard Christians say, "I get to know God best in nature." The problem with that statement is that if nature is all you have, you are missing out on the *depth* with which He intends for you to know Him. God gave even the heathens revelation in nature. If you are only pursuing God in nature, you'll end up settling for the heathens' portion. We'll never be satisfied with a universal knowledge of God. We want a personal knowledge, a relational knowledge, because God is a relational being, not just an energy force in the cosmos. That is what God desires and why His Book was given to His children.

Jesus had just finished telling a parable to the multitudes. "The disciples came to him and asked, 'Why do you speak to the people in parables?' He replied, 'The knowledge of the secrets of the kingdom of heaven has been given to you, but not to them'" (Matthew 13:10–11). Do you hear what Jesus was saying? *The knowledge of the secrets of the kingdom of heaven* has been given to us. These secrets are ours. They belong to us. What are we doing with them? Do we even know what they are? Do we want to know the secrets of the kingdom of heaven? They're found in His Word.

One more verse I must include: "He who forms the mountains, creates the wind, and *reveals his thoughts to man*, he who turns dawn to darkness, and treads the high places of the earth—the LORD God Almighty is his name" (Amos 4:13, emphasis added). The same God who created the mountains and the wind has chosen to reveal His thoughts to man. Why? Because He wants us to know Him! Where has God revealed these thoughts? In the pages of the Bible. Yet because of our depraved nature, we want to find God on our own; we want to do it our way.

Some people even make the Bible their last resort. They'd rather learn about God from their pastor, a radio preacher, worshipful songs, or a suspenseful Christian novel. I know—I've been there! I have also robbed myself of many years of deep intimacy with God because much of what I was learning about Him was secondhand. I was depending on others to spoon-feed me.

As we get to know God one-on-one, we are given the inside track on becoming His friend. On the night that Jesus was betrayed, He assembled with His disciples and told them, "I no longer call you servants, because a servant does not know his master's business. Instead, I have called you friends, for everything that I learned from my Father I have made known to you" (John 15:15). Why did Jesus say that He was now calling them friends? Because He had told them everything about the family business. He had shared with them His background and His future. He had revealed His mission and the calling on His life. He had given them *knowledge.* That was the difference.

My closest friends have the inside scoop on me. They know my heart and my passion. They know what makes me tick and what rattles my cage. They know my deepest thoughts and secrets. The closer the friend, the more he or she knows. My friends know me because I have let them in. I have revealed myself to them. No one can be my friend unless I give that person access.

The same is true with God. We know from the Bible that God chose to reveal Himself to certain people, such as Abraham, Joseph, and Moses. Not only did they *know about* God, they *experienced companionship* with God. They walked with God, and His presence was manifested to them. This was God's doing. He chose to let them know Him, to let them be acquainted with Him. And their lives were unique because they knew God as one knows a friend. God wants all of His children to know Him in this way, to be His friend.

Jesus said, "You are my friends if you do what I command" (John 15:14). Just a few years ago, I would have been reluctant to call myself God's friend. It would have seemed so presumptuous, so bold. But now I wouldn't hesitate because I know Him and I am obeying Him daily. It is not arrogant or audacious for me to consider myself God's friend. *He* calls me friend, and so I am!

Jesus has called me friend. He has invited me into His inner circle. He is pursuing an intimate relationship with me. He is my comrade and my confidant. He lets me pour out my heart to Him, and He discloses His heart to me. He reveals His thoughts page after page. He has written down His expressions of love for me, His intentions for my highest good, and His unwavering commitment to my future. Our special relationship has blossomed into something far beyond what I have ever known. He has become more real to me and more dear to me than anything life could offer. My loving relationship with my Abba Father is my greatest treasure. This is what pursuing the knowledge of God has done for me.

Memorizing Scripture kept pointing me to God's character, my need, and the safety of being with Him. As each new year has brought laughter and tears, God has been my focus and His Word my anchor. One particular year when life was a challenge just to survive, I memorized Psalm 62 in the midst of my struggle. Here is a portion of that psalm.

> *My soul finds rest in God alone;*
> *my salvation comes from him.*
> *He alone is my rock and my salvation;*
> *he is my fortress, I will never be shaken.*
> ∽ Psalm 62:1–2

In order for me to memorize this passage, I had to say it over and over and over. I had to dwell on each phrase, each term. These words spoke life to me. They reminded me of God's tenderness toward me and His provision for my helplessness. They were God's invitation to come to Him, cling to Him, and find my solace in His arms. I come to this psalm often. I have to. I *need* to. Its truth is my comfort and strength and keeps me running back to my Father, my Friend who waits for me.

Do you want to be God's friend? Do you want Him to let you in on the secrets of heaven and earth? Do you yearn to know intimately the God who created you? God our Father has already told us in His Word everything He wants us to know about Him. He has chosen to reveal Himself to us. The ball is now in our court. We decide how much we want to know, how close a friend we want to be. God told the people of Israel, "You will seek Me and find Me when you search for Me with all your heart. I will be found by you" (Jeremiah 29:13–14 NASB). God will let us find Him, but our part is to get into His Word. We will find Him there.

Many Christians carry around misconceptions about knowledge. Here's an example. In the past few years, God has given me many opportunities to speak in various places, reciting one of the books of the Bible I know from memory. A comment made to me frequently is, "You will be the one thrown into prison for your faith because you know God's Word." I cannot tell you how many people have said this to me. At first I was puzzled by these comments. It was as if they were afraid to know God's Word because terrible things might happen to them. Then I realized how ridiculous this thinking was. It was like saying, "Because you wear your seat belt, you'll be the one in the car accident." No, just because I wear my seat belt doesn't destine me for a car accident, but if I'm in one I'll be more prepared. Just because I have some of God's Word memorized does not make me a candidate for religious imprisonment.

That is just one example of the misconceptions people have about knowledge. Some people are obviously afraid of too much knowledge. Some revere knowledge unduly, whereas others dismiss it as inconsequential. Many are turned off by knowledge because of a deep disappointment in someone they knew who had abundant knowledge of the Bible, maybe even preached God's Word, and yet whose life told a different story. And so we ask, "What did knowledge do for him?" We conclude that knowing the Bible is not the answer. I, too, have been disillusioned by knowledgeable people who have failed. I've had two pastors resign their pastorates because of adultery, and another who resigned because of divorce. Each time, I was hurt, angry, and frustrated. How could this have happened to a man of God, a man of God's Word?

Many want to throw out knowledge when something like this happens. But we must not resist or reject knowledge. Being knowledgeable and being spiritually mature are not always one and the same. Head knowledge is not necessarily heart knowledge. However, our growth and maturity depend heavily on our knowledge and what we do with that knowledge. We should avoid either extreme—venerating knowledge beyond its worth or minimizing its value. Knowledge is not irrelevant. Ignorance is not bliss.

Jesus said we are to love God with all parts of the human personality. To love Him with all our hearts, we must give Him all our affection and all our adoration, having no other love before Him. To love God with all our souls, we must surrender our very lives, all that we are. To love God with all our strength, we must give every effort to demonstrate our love by our obedience. To love God with all our minds partly means loving

Him with all our brain's capacity, pursuing with our minds the one true God, making Him first over all other intellectual preoccupations. It means choosing to align our minds with His.

Memorizing Scripture will help us do all of this. Once we have selected a passage to memorize and have begun saying the words, we are trading our thoughts for God's. We are chasing after truth, God's truth. We are choosing to embrace the God of the Bible rather than the god in our own minds. We are finding our delight in knowing God. We are confirming our love for God each day by persisting in the search for true knowledge. We are saying to God, "I want to know You so that I can love You more."

Memorizing Scripture holds our minds captive so that we can focus on God and His thoughts. It disciplines our minds so that we can learn the things we want to know. What I was not expecting was to learn so many things I *didn't* want to know. When we memorize passages or books, there are inevitably parts we would not otherwise choose to memorize. Second Peter 2 was full of such verses, but it was sandwiched between chapters 1 and 3, so I was stuck. I didn't care much for chapter 2, but God used it to impress upon me the wickedness of false teachers and their impending judgment. Every time I review that book, I am reminded of God's no-tolerance attitude toward those who lead others astray. Memorizing passages and chapters has helped to ground me in truths I wasn't necessarily eager to know but that God wanted me to understand.

About twenty years ago, when I was single and carefree, I had a concerned friend who wanted to teach my two roommates and me how to change a tire in case we were ever stranded. That was not how I had envisioned spending my Saturday afternoon, and being the optimistic person I was, I couldn't imagine ever needing this information. But he insisted, and so we participated in the training session to appease our paranoid friend. It was a long, hot, laborious exercise, especially considering that "we were never going to need this."

Two short years after this "educational workshop," I was in desperate need of that knowledge. While I was driving on the interstate in Orlando with my mother, we heard an explosion, and she exclaimed, "Oh, dear, I think we've blown a tire." With dubious confidence I said, "No problem, Mother. I know how to change a tire!" Actually, my plan was just to appear like we were getting started, and surely by then, those helpful highway patrolmen would rescue us. Step one was climbing into the trunk with my dress on to hoist the spare tire out. Some forty-five minutes later, one of those uniformed gentlemen showed up. "You ladies need any help?" I replied, "Thank you very much, but we have just changed our own tire; no chivalry needed." The point of this tale is that stored information, though not immediately useful, can become beneficial at a later date. This is often true of Scripture. It is always valuable but not always at the time you expect it to be valuable.

That is why I memorize Scripture with my two teenagers on the way to school each morning. I know with absolute certainty that God's Word will be faithful to achieve His purposes in their lives. The knowledge they gain will penetrate their minds and hearts, and God will remind them of these truths later, when they need them. During the fall semester we memorized Proverbs 2. I wanted them to have no doubt about the source of all wisdom and understanding and to motivate them to go after it. I also wanted to warn them to stay on the right path because of dangers that lie ahead. Here are a few of the verses:

My son, if you accept my words
and store up my commands within you,
turning your ear to wisdom
and applying your heart to understanding,
and if you call out for insight
and cry aloud for understanding,
and if you look for it as for silver
and search for it as for hidden treasure,
then you will understand the fear of the LORD
and find the knowledge of God.
For the LORD *gives wisdom,*
and from his mouth come knowledge and understanding.
He holds victory in store for the upright,
he is a shield to those whose walk is blameless,
for he guards the course of the just
and protects the way of his faithful ones.

Then you will understand what is right and just
and fair—every good path.
For wisdom will enter your heart,
and knowledge will be pleasant to your soul.
∞ Proverbs 2:1–10, emphasis added

I know of nothing more pleasurable to the human soul than the knowledge of God. To know God and His Word has been the joy of my heart and the delight of my life. My daily communion with my Father, rehearsing His words over and over, has given me so much pleasure. When my soul is thriving, it lends perspective to everything else, and I am able to handle the pressures and crises of life.

In Proverbs 2, the Scriptures identify the benefits of accepting and storing up God's Word: wisdom, knowledge, and understanding. There is no debate that life can be inscrutably complex at times. The formidable challenge of raising a family in a culture increasingly hostile to Christian principles is intimidating. That is why I am storing up knowledge and trusting that God will give me wisdom and understanding to guide me through the maze.

Proverbs 24:3–4 says, "By wisdom a house is built, and through understanding it is established; through knowledge its rooms are filled with rare and beautiful treasures." What a stirring depiction: building our household on the foundation of God's wisdom and truth, and filling each room with the knowledge of God.

When people come into your home, are they impacted by the knowledge of God in that place? Can they sense God's presence, or does worldly clutter make Him difficult to see? Do they hear His words, or is there contentious clamoring drowning out His voice?

> O God,
> Make our homes a sanctuary where all who enter
> will find truth. Build a lasting foundation through
> wisdom and understanding.
> Fill each room with the knowledge of You.

Keep Your words flowing through our homes,
giving life . . . and hope . . . and pleasure.
Amen.

The heart of the discerning acquires knowledge;
the ears of the wise seek it out.
∽ Proverbs 18:15

5

Your Turn:

ONE WHO LOVES
WHAT IS GOOD

ou are now ready for your next opportunity, since you breezed right through Psalm 1. We're going to take on the book of Titus, a letter that is rich in truth for practical living. Before I memorized this book, I could not have told you what was in it, even though I had read it many times. Might this also be true for you, that there are some books you have read dozens of times and yet you couldn't give a brief summary of what is in them? I guarantee that after memorizing the book of Titus, or any other book, you will never forget the content, even if you forget the word-for-word text. I have learned many books this way, and those are my greatest treasures. Confidence in knowing the Bible is one of the benefits I have reaped by this same process. Titus has forty-six verses in three chapters. You'll be absolutely amazed at how much you can learn from one small book.

I've acquired a few tips along the way that I'm happy to pass along. Before you begin with the memorizing, you'll need to write out your chapter on your index card spiral. It is always a great motivation for me to see ahead of time what I am going to be learning. You don't have to do this in one sitting. Fit it in whenever you can. Use the same spiral that contains Psalm 1. At least for now you'll only have one spiral to keep track of. To separate the different passages, I change the color of ink for each chapter. That way I can quickly find where I am in the Scripture text when I 'm driving or on the walking track. As before, keep your reference numbers at the far left, so you'll know where you need to be. (Don't worry; we're not going to memorize the numbers.)

To simplify the process, I always start a new chapter on the first day of a month. This makes it easier to remember what verse I am on. For example, if it is May 12, I know I am on verse 12. You will have enough to remember without fretting over what verse you are supposed to be on. Feel free to devise your own system that works for you and your lifestyle. For our purposes now, don't wait until the first of the month. There's no better time than today. I will walk you through the first ten days. Now you're ready to begin.

Day One

:1 PAUL, A SERVANT OF GOD AND AN APOSTLE
    OF JESUS CHRIST
FOR THE FAITH OF GOD'S ELECT
AND THE KNOWLEDGE OF THE TRUTH THAT
LEADS TO GODLINESS—

∞ No matter what day it is, what time it is, or what your day holds, you will be spending some time getting ready for the day: showering, drying your hair, putting on your makeup, getting dressed, fixing breakfast and coffee, making school lunches. Including Scripture memory as part of your morning routine will help to make it a permanent part of your life. It's also an energizing way to start your day that will not take any extra time.

∞ Start with the first verse. Say it out loud again and again.

∞ Move segment by segment until you think you have it—about ten or fifteen times.

∞ This one verse will take approximately eight seconds to review.

∞ Look at it again while making breakfast. The toaster takes longer than reciting this verse.

∞ Share it with your spouse or your kids, even if they're only two years old. They'll love it!

∞ Prop up your index spiral on the ironing board while you iron.

∞ Take your spiral with you in the car on the way to work or to school.

∞ Turn the radio off and consider what the verse is saying.

∞ Who? *Paul.* How does he describe himself? *A servant of God and an apostle of Jesus Christ.*

∞ Why is he writing? *For the faith of God's elect and the knowledge of the truth.*

∞ Where does the knowledge of the truth lead? *It leads to godliness.*

∞ Is this what you want? *Yes.* Then go after truth. That's why we're doing this.

∞ There is so much in this one verse. Think about it. Pray about it. Let it come alive in you.

∞ Review this one verse throughout your day.

∞ Come back to it as often as you can. Remember, it only takes eight seconds at this point.

Day Two

:2 A FAITH AND KNOWLEDGE
RESTING ON THE HOPE OF ETERNAL LIFE,
WHICH GOD, WHO DOES NOT LIE,
PROMISED BEFORE THE BEGINNING OF TIME,

∞ Begin reviewing verse 1 first thing in the morning.

∞ Review it in the shower. See if you remember it from yesterday.

∞ Move on to verse 2.

∞ Say verses 1 and 2 out loud, line by line, until you have them by heart.

∞ It doesn't matter if this takes ten or fifteen times. This is normal.

∾ Today, throughout your day, these two verses are your focus.

∾ Think about what the verse is saying. Chew on it in your mind.

∾ Ask questions: Who, what, where, when, why, and how.

∾ Where is my faith resting? *On the hope of eternal life.*

∾ Who promised this? *God.*

∾ When? *Before the beginning of time.*

∾ What attribute of God is mentioned? *He does not lie.* Wow!

∾ How sure is your faith? *As sure as God Himself.*

∾ Think about this all day long. Let the richness of this truth consume your thoughts.

Day Three

:3 AND AT HIS APPOINTED SEASON
HE BROUGHT HIS WORD TO LIGHT
THROUGH THE PREACHING ENTRUSTED TO ME
BY THE COMMAND OF GOD OUR SAVIOR,

∾ Review verses 1 and 2 as soon as you get up. Try to do this without looking, and see if you have it.

∾ Move on to verse 3. Take it line by line. Say it with the other verses.

∽ Can you see that even now, at God's appointed season, He is bringing His Word to light for you through Paul's teaching in the book of Titus? Thank God for all you are learning.

∽ Don't forget to review Psalm 1, if this is your designated day.

∽ Verses 1 through 3 of Titus 1 will take about twenty-five seconds to review. Look for opportunities to squeeze it in.

∽ Come back to God's Word at the end of the day. Thank God for this incredible gift.

Day Four

:4 TO TITUS,
MY TRUE SON IN OUR COMMON FAITH:
GRACE AND PEACE FROM GOD THE FATHER
AND CHRIST JESUS OUR SAVIOR.

∽ As soon as you wake up, direct your thoughts toward God's Word. Review your three verses.

∽ Start today's verse. Break it down phrase by phrase. Say all four verses together.

∽ Identify times in your day when your hands are busy but your mind is free: as you fold the laundry, empty the dishwasher, vacuum the house, boil water, wait on-hold.

∽ Push the mute button during commercials. You know how long commercials are.

∽ Don't let your mind be idle. Seize those moments for God's Word.

∽ Are you working out on a treadmill or an exercise bike? Exercise your mind at the same time.

∽ Conclude your day by meditating on God's Word. How blessed you will be!

Day Five

:5 THE REASON I LEFT YOU IN CRETE
WAS THAT YOU MIGHT STRAIGHTEN OUT WHAT WAS LEFT
UNFINISHED
AND APPOINT ELDERS IN EVERY TOWN,
AS I DIRECTED YOU.

∽ Begin your day by focusing on God's Word. Review your previous verses.

∽ Add today's verse. Say it out loud. You will be up to about forty-five seconds.

∽ Paul is now giving his purpose for writing this letter. Ask God to give you insights.

∽ Prop up your index spiral in the bathroom while you get ready for the day. Then take it to the kitchen.

∽ Leave it sitting up in a place you will pass by several times a day as a reminder to review.

∽ Will you be walking today, or jogging, or pushing the baby in the stroller? Use that time.

∞ While you're cooking supper, steer your mind back to God's Word.

∞ Can you sense God disciplining your mind to focus on Him?

∞ Give your last few moments before bed to think about your verses in Titus.

Day Six

:6 AN ELDER MUST BE BLAMELESS,
THE HUSBAND OF BUT ONE WIFE,
A MAN WHOSE CHILDREN BELIEVE
AND ARE NOT OPEN TO THE CHARGE OF BEING WILD
    AND DISOBEDIENT.

∞ I assume you're in the habit now of giving your first thoughts of the day to God.

∞ Don't miss even one day. It makes such a difference in your outlook.

∞ Paul is now giving Titus the qualifications for elders, leaders of the church.

∞ Review your previous verses and then add today's verse.

∞ As you go about your day, meditate on what you have learned so far.

∞ Are you running errands today? Take your verses with you.

    ∞ Review while you're waiting at the bank drive-through, the post office, and the red light.

    ∞ When your mind gets tired, just read the verses. You are still reinforcing the words.

Day Seven

:7 SINCE AN OVERSEER IS ENTRUSTED WITH GOD'S WORK,
HE MUST BE BLAMELESS—NOT OVERBEARING,
NOT QUICK-TEMPERED, NOT GIVEN TO DRUNKENNESS,
NOT VIOLENT, NOT PURSUING DISHONEST GAIN.

    ∞ Even if you're not a morning person, memorizing God's Word makes getting up more pleasant.

    ∞ Go over your verses in the shower. See if you're on target so far.

    ∞ Add today's verse. Learn it word by word, phrase by phrase, or line by line.

    ∞ Think about why God included these as qualifications for leadership in the church. The answer is in the word *since.* Have you also been entrusted with God's work? Think about it.

    ∞ Share what you are learning with your children. They need to know these things, and it will only take a minute or two. How will they know unless you tell them? Don't count on someone else.

    ∞ What are you doing today that will let you fit in a minute to practice? Are you sweeping the front porch, raking leaves, doing some gardening, mowing the lawn, or taking the dog for a walk?

Day Eight

:8 RATHER HE MUST BE HOSPITABLE,
ONE WHO LOVES WHAT IS GOOD,
WHO IS SELF-CONTROLLED,
UPRIGHT, HOLY AND DISCIPLINED.

> ∞ A new day and a new verse. Review your other verses first and then tackle the new one.

> ∞ Are the qualities listed only for elders, or does God want each of us to attain to these standards?

> ∞ Are you pursuing these? Ask God to build them into your life.

> ∞ What mother doesn't need the character described here?

> ∞ Meditate on this list throughout your day. Let it roll over and over in your mind.

> ∞ Don't miss what God is saying to you. Make each line a prayer.

> ∞ By working on these verses throughout your day, you are training and disciplining your mind.

Day Nine

:9 HE MUST HOLD FIRMLY TO THE TRUSTWORTHY MESSAGE
AS IT HAS BEEN TAUGHT,
SO THAT HE CAN ENCOURAGE OTHERS BY SOUND DOCTRINE
AND REFUTE THOSE WHO OPPOSE IT.

> ∞ As soon as you open your eyes for the new

day, let your thoughts run to God's Word.

∽ Your review of verses 1 through 8 will take about one minute.

∽ Go over verses 1–8 a few times before you start your next verse. Take the new verse, line by line.

∽ What is the message here? Ask yourself, *What must he do, and why?* Is this also for you?

∽ A Christian leader must be familiar with God's message so that he can encourage others with God's Word and defend truth to those who are antagonistic. You may not have arrived yet, but you are on your way. Do not turn back.

Day Ten

:10 FOR THERE ARE MANY REBELLIOUS PEOPLE, MERE TALKERS AND DECEIVERS, ESPECIALLY THOSE OF THE CIRCUMCISION GROUP.

∽ Maintain the discipline of putting God's Word first in your day. Review what you have learned so far.

∽ Move on when you are ready. Today's verse gives the reason for verse 9.

∽ Do we find people like this today? Yes, and *we're all vulnerable to their influence.*

∞ As you repeat this verse, cry out to God, asking Him to keep you from becoming one of them.

∞ Share your progress with someone who would be edified. Ask that person to check up on you later.

∞ Give the final moments of your day to God. Rehearse His Word as you drift off to sleep.

Day Eleven

:11 THEY MUST BE SILENCED,
BECAUSE THEY ARE RUINING WHOLE HOUSEHOLDS
BY TEACHING THINGS THEY OUGHT NOT TO TEACH—
AND THAT FOR THE SAKE OF DISHONEST GAIN.

Day Twelve

:12 EVEN ONE OF THEIR OWN PROPHETS HAS SAID,
"CRETANS ARE ALWAYS LIARS,
EVIL BRUTES, LAZY GLUTTONS."

Day Thirteen

:13 THIS TESTIMONY IS TRUE.
THEREFORE, REBUKE THEM SHARPLY,
SO THAT THEY WILL BE SOUND IN THE FAITH

Day Fourteen

:14 AND WILL PAY NO ATTENTION TO JEWISH MYTHS
OR TO THE COMMANDS OF THOSE
WHO REJECT THE TRUTH.

Day Fifteen

:15 TO THE PURE, ALL THINGS ARE PURE,
BUT TO THOSE WHO ARE CORRUPTED AND DO NOT BELIEVE,
NOTHING IS PURE.
IN FACT, BOTH THEIR MINDS AND CONSCIENCES ARE
    CORRUPTED.

Day Sixteen

:16 THEY CLAIM TO KNOW GOD,
BUT BY THEIR ACTIONS THEY DENY HIM.
THEY ARE DETESTABLE, DISOBEDIENT
AND UNFIT FOR DOING ANYTHING GOOD.

You made it. You've finished an entire chapter. Wow! Don't you feel great? Something significant is taking place in your life. You are being trained to give your free thoughts to God instead of to daydreaming. You are redeeming the time that might have been wasted. Now you are planted by streams of water, and you are drinking deeply. I'm so proud of you. Discipline comes at a price, but, oh, the rewards!

A FEW TIPS

∞ Just as you did for Psalm 1, pick a day of the week and designate it for the book of Titus. For example, Tuesday might be the day that you will always review Titus. While working on chapter 2, review chapter 1 on Tuesdays. While working on chapter 3, review chapters 1 and 2 on Tuesdays. No matter what other passages you go on to memorize, you will always review Titus on

Tuesdays. That will be fifty-two times a year. As you add other books and passages, you'll be gaining a storehouse of knowledge that you can draw from when needed.

∞ Before you begin Titus 2, take the next few days just for review of chapter 1, so that you can solidify this chapter in your mind before you move on. The entire chapter will take approximately two minutes to review. By now you are convinced that you can find two-minute segments in your day. If your mind begins wandering to other things because you have mastered these verses and don't need to review them anymore, then it's time to start chapter 2. In chapter 7 we will go through Titus 2–3.

∞ While you are reviewing Titus 1, ask yourself questions that will help you summarize the content. *Why was Paul writing to Titus? What type of men was Titus to look for to lead the churches? And why? What were the problems Titus was facing? What are the obvious contrasts in this chapter?* These questions and others will cause you to think about the message, not just repeat the words. And most important, ask, *How does God want me to apply these truths in my life?* Be still and let God speak to you. Ask Him to keep His words alive in your heart, transforming you into "one who loves what is good."

You will find that the discipline of memorizing Scripture becomes more automatic the more you do it. Each time you capture those idle moments for God's Word, you are conditioning yourself and producing self-governing habits. And you will be attaining your ultimate goal of keeping your focus on God throughout your day, in the midst of life's other demands.

I have been taking my two teenagers to the orthodontist once a month for the last four years, two years each. Instead of sitting in the waiting room listening to secular music and reading tacky magazines, I often wait outside in my car, going over my verses. You can cover a lot of territory in thirty to forty-five minutes. This is just one example that has worked for me. It wouldn't work with a three-year-old. You will find your own pockets of time as you look for them.

Time is a precious commodity, with only twenty-four hours allotted to each one of us each day. I am not by nature an efficient time manager, but I have learned to utilize little moments here and there for God's Word. Though two-minute slots may have seemed insignificant at the time I began memorizing, they have added up to an enormous amount of Scripture memorized in ten years. I am now working on my ninety-first chapter. I do not share that to overwhelm you, but to show you that great progress comes a few minutes at a time.

Before we get sidetracked from our purpose, let me assure you that there will be no checklist or prize at the pearly gates for the number of verses quoted. What matters is a life that has been transformed by the sword of God's Word penetrating deep into our souls and making us more pliable and yielding to His will. It matters not what is stored in our minds if it is not also written on our hearts.

> *Oh, how I love your law!*
> *I meditate on it all day long.*
> ∞ Psalm 119:97

6
Benefit #2:

TO OBEY IS BETTER
THAN SACRIFICE

Saul, Israel's first king, was given some instructions from God through Samuel the prophet. "Now go, attack the Amalekites and totally destroy everything that belongs to them. Do not spare them; put to death men and women, children and infants, cattle and sheep, camels and donkeys" (1 Samuel 15:3).

So Saul and his men went out and attacked the Amalekites. "But Saul and the army spared Agag and the best of the sheep and cattle, the fat calves and lambs—everything that was good. These they were unwilling to destroy completely, but everything that was despised and weak they totally destroyed" (v. 9).

Saul then told Samuel that he had carried out God's instructions. Samuel asked, "What then is this bleating of sheep in my ears?" (v. 14). Saul explained that they had saved the best animals to sacrifice to the Lord. Samuel's memorable response to all this:

> *"Does the LORD delight in burnt offerings and sacrifices*
> *as much as in obeying the voice of the LORD?*
> *To obey is better than sacrifice,*
> *and to heed is better than the fat of rams. . . .*
> *Because you have rejected the word of the LORD,*
> *he has rejected you as king."*
> ∞ 1 Samuel 15:22–23

God is serious about obedience, even to the point of removing a king who compromised. God requires obedience. He commands it. He demands it. He does not negotiate for mutual concessions.

God already has a perfect plan for the world, His kingdom, and me. This plan cannot be improved upon. Now, what He wants from me, His child, is unaltered obedience. This makes so much sense when I think about my own children. When they were small, and I told them to pick up their toys and put them away, I did not want to walk into their room and find them coloring a picture for me. I wanted them to pick up their toys. Now, with my teenagers, if I tell them to be home at eleven o'clock, I don't want to hear that they were late because they stopped at Wal-Mart to buy me a gift. I want them *to be home at eleven o'clock!* Why is this concept so clear when we relate it to *our* children, but so clouded when *we* are the children? Because our sin nature cries out for independence; we want to do it our way. On top of that, we are wise in our own eyes and somehow think we have a better plan than God!

When our son Austin was born, one foot was bent the wrong way. We were sent to a specialist, who explained that it was a completely normal foot but had been cramped in the womb. This doctor did not ask for our suggestions or ideas; he had his own procedure. He described the tiny orthopedic shoes Austin would have to wear. These would hold both of his feet together with an eight-inch metal brace. The doctor assured us that if we followed his instructions precisely, Austin would have a perfect foot in about a year, with no lasting effects. If we didn't follow his orders, Austin would be impaired for the rest of his life.

The instructions were simple: Keep the shoes on at all times, except for bathing, and buy new shoes every four or five weeks. That didn't sound too complicated. We left the doctor's office with our six-week-old baby boy and his new shoes. We were so relieved at the good news and determined to be faithful to the guidelines because nothing less than a perfect foot was acceptable for our son.

Before we even pulled into our driveway, Austin began to cry. He did not like those pretty new shoes. His feet were basically tied together, and he couldn't kick one without the other. He cried, he screamed, he got mad, he fought and kicked and begged us with his eyes to stop this torture. He didn't understand what was happening to him and why we were being so cruel. He looked at us with such sad eyes, and we really did feel sorry for him. But we loved him too much to give in, no matter how much he cried. That first day and night, he wailed constantly until he was so exhausted he finally fell asleep.

The next day, we were flying to Florida to visit

grandparents, so we decided to skip the bath that morning, because if we took off the shoes and he tasted freedom, he'd start crying again when we put them back on. We went to Florida, and it wasn't until the next day that we finally took the shoes off for the first time to bathe him. Bless his heart, he had kicked and fought so much that he had a terrible blister on his heel, already broken, sore, and red. It was almost too much for a mother to bear.

I called the doctor in Dallas and asked if we could keep the shoes off until it healed. He said, "Absolutely not. If it hurts him enough, he'll quit kicking." For the next twelve months, we rigidly followed the doctor's orders, and today our son has a perfect foot. He said to me the other day, "Mom, which foot was it?" I laughed and said, "I can't even remember."

What's the point to this story? We are all born defective, and God, who is the Master Designer, has a plan to fix us. He has given us a Book of complete instructions, and He has given us a resident Helper, His Spirit. As we obey these instructions, we are being transformed to conform to God's original design. If we ignore the instructions, we will continue to be impaired. When we are faced with these two options, there seems an obvious choice, but of course, it's never that simple. Obedience means changing, and we resist change because it is often a painful process that involves trials and hardships. Our nature tells us to find another way so that we can avoid the bruises and scars. We may kick and scream and blame God, but *He loves us too much to change the instructions.* Nothing less than perfect is acceptable to God because we are His children.

God also has a plan for the world, and He is allowing us to be a part of it. This plan was designed with no detail left unnoticed. There is nothing we could recommend that He has not already thought of. He's not asking for our advice or our opinion. He's asking for our obedience.

What is mind-boggling is that God's perfect plan for me and God's perfect plan for the world are intertwined, so that He doesn't have to sacrifice the good of one for the good of the other. God's intentions for me cannot be foiled by His intentions for someone else or His intentions for the universe. Wow! Our finite minds cannot fathom the sovereignty of God or the inner workings of His will. But we know from His Word that His plans will ultimately succeed, with or without our enthusiastic participation. God and His ways will prevail above all else.

Man's own human will and human plans are of no eternal significance unless they coincide with God's will. Although this truth may seem obvious, it took me years to come to grips with it. Now that I am thoroughly convinced of this truth, I don't want to waste any time on my plans and my will. I want to get in on God's flawless plans that are destined to succeed and forget my plans that are destined to fail. How do I go about doing this?

Listen to what God said to Joshua as the new leader of Israel.

> *"Be careful to obey all the law my servant Moses gave you; do not turn from it to the right or to the left, that you may be successful wherever you go. Do not let this Book of the Law depart from your mouth; meditate on it day and night, so that you may be careful to do everything written in it. Then you will be prosperous and successful."*
>
> ∞ Joshua 1:7–8

Now don't miss this important point. The key to
Joshua's success was *not* meditating on God's Word. The
key to Joshua's success was obedience. It was *obedience* to
God's Word, to do everything written in it. OK, what
could he do to *ensure* his obedience? Two things were
mentioned:

1. God's Law should always be on his mouth.

2. He should meditate on God's Law day and
   night.

Those principles apply to us today. If we are continually talking about and thinking about God's Law,
we will be more careful to obey and less likely to stray
to the right or to the left. Did you notice that God did
not say, "This Law should always be *at your side*" (as in
carrying your Bible to and from church and leaving it
on the car seat next to you)? We must keep it *on our lips.*

The outcome of Joshua's obedience would be prosperity and success. In today's culture, prosperity and
success mean economic gain, but this was not what
God was referring to when He spoke to Joshua. The
Hebrew word for "prosperous" indicates "to push forward."[1] The Hebrew word for "success" means "to be
circumspect, be prudent."[2] The outcome of Joshua's
obedience was the advancement of God's program in a
careful and circumspect manner. In other words, Joshua
would know what to do in a given situation in order to
further God's agenda. A pattern of obedience makes us
wise in our choice of action.

Since it is only obedience to God's will and God's

Word that will succeed, then we must do *whatever it takes* to keep us obedient. Never mind listening to the world or to those entangled in the world; they will not lead us to obedience. God tells us that constantly talking about and meditating on His Word day and night will help us to obey.

This is where I have found the discipline of memorizing Scripture invaluable. Saying God's Word over and over throughout each day has resulted in more obedience in my life in particular areas and specific situations. I have experienced the piercing of His double-edged sword, going deep into my soul, exposing hidden motives, and revealing the wretched nature I've been concealing all my life. God is exposing those areas so that they can be removed.

One such area in which I have seen tremendous progress is in loving what the Bible calls "the things of the world," which, in this case, I'm taking literally. This has been a great struggle for me—because I admit it—I love things! I love pretty things. I love expensive things. I love buying things for people. I love buying things for myself. So what's the problem? God's Word tells us:

> *Do not love the world or anything in the world. If anyone loves the world, the love of the Father is not in him. For everything in the world—the cravings of sinful man, the lust of his eyes and the boasting of what he has and does—comes not from the Father but from the world. The world and its desires pass away, but the man who does the will of God lives forever.*
> ∽ 1 John 2:15–17, emphasis added

When I began to memorize the book of 1 John, I could see what was coming, and I knew I would have to deal with it. I said these words again and again, repeating them to myself and making them a plea to the Lord to change me. When God's Word told me that if I loved the world and its things, then I did not love Him, it broke my heart. I found myself sighing, moaning, shaking my head, and saying, "I don't want to love the world."

I agonized about this because I knew it was an area of weakness that had to be worked on. How could I be all that God wanted me to be if my affections were divided? God's Word spoke the truth to me, and I couldn't escape it. It gave me the desire to change and the courage to see it through. I can honestly say that I do not love the world or material things the way I used to, though this will probably always be an area of vulnerability for me. Sometimes I am tempted to love the world or the things it promises, but now I know where to go for help. I don't even have to look up the words. They're stored in my mind, and God is in the process of writing them on my heart.

God's Word is able to do the same for you. It is not likely that, after spending weeks and months looking to God, reciting His words, and thinking His thoughts day in, day out, you would want to go out and recklessly discredit Him by your life. It is more probable that your desire would be to honor God and live worthy of His name. Meditating on God's Word day and night germinates a longing within us to live up to His Word.

You and I have experienced both *willful* obedience and *willing* obedience, preferring the latter as the more enjoyable route. Each is legitimate and acceptable to God. If we choose to obey as an act of our will, even though we don't want to, this willful obedience is nonetheless sufficient; we are being obedient. Willful obedience can lead to *willing* obedience. When I eagerly yield to God's commands, this willing obedience is often because I have been persuaded to His point of view. This persuasion comes from God's Word.

For example, my role as a wife is to submit to the leadership and direction of my husband. Two specific passages of Scripture I have memorized address this issue.

> *Wives, in the same way be submissive to your husbands so that, if any of them do not believe the word, they may be won over without words by the behavior of their wives, when they see the purity and reverence of your lives.*
>
> ∞ 1 Peter 3:1–2

> *Wives, submit to your husbands as to the Lord. For the husband is the head of the wife as Christ is head of the church, his body, of which he is the Savior. Now as the church submits to Christ, so also wives should submit to their husbands* in everything.
>
> ∞ Ephesians 5:22–24, emphasis added

Having learned these verses years ago, and being committed to review them regularly, I have said these verses out loud hundreds of times. I tell you candidly that this concept has never been easy for me to implement, especially the word *everything.* I often wrestle with this command and may never conquer the struggle. However, I have become convinced that this is God's way and therefore the best way. Knowing this and having a deep conviction that it is true compels me to obey, even when I don't want to, even if it has to be sheer, willful obedience.

I've heard people say, "I didn't continue with such and such because I was only doing it out of duty, and God knew I really didn't want to." Well, what's wrong with duty? It's a stepping-stone to doing something because you want to. When I ask my son to take out the garbage, I don't really care if he wants to or not. I want it done—now. Sure, I'd like a smile on his face, but either way will suffice. Will he eventually want to take out the garbage because of his immense appreciation for all I have done for him? Probably so, but he will have moved out by then.

As we teach our children the things we are learning from God's Word, they will be watching us to see if we are obeying God. For example, if we teach our children, "Do not let any unwholesome talk come out of your mouths" (Ephesians 4:29) but then get on the phone and gossip with our friends, we've just erased what we told them. Instead, we have modeled to them that *knowing* God's Word is important but not *obeying* it. They're watching us more than we realize, and when they become teenagers they will tune us out if they see hypocrisy. That is a sobering thought!

The example we want to model for our children is *not* that obeying God is always what we want to do but that obeying God is what we *must* do, even when we don't want to. Obeying God is not always easy, but it's always right. Such is the difficult task of imperfect mothers trying to train up children in the way they should go. If they don't see a pattern of obedience in our lives, our words will be in vain.

And so we ask, "How do we get from where we are to where we want to be?" In our relationship with God, there is a natural progression from *knowledge* to *intimacy* to *obedience*. The more I know Him, the more I love Him. The more I love Him, the greater my desire to please Him, which means obeying Him. This obedience then leads back to two things: more knowledge of Him and a more intimate relationship with Him.

Jesus explains this to His disciples. In John 13–17, we find Jesus' final words to His disciples. These eleven men Jesus had chosen to be with Him during His earthly ministry (Judas had already left to seek out the high priest and betray Jesus). What did Jesus say to them on their final evening together? He told them about an essential ingredient to intimacy with Him, how to keep their love relationship with Him going, even though He was leaving them to go back to His Father.

Jesus revealed to them the true test of their love for Him. Why did He have to do this? These men had known the command to love God all their lives. Jesus had to tell them specifically because He knew their tendency to make up their own definitions. We do the same. We like to decide for ourselves how we want to love God. Someone might say something like "Of course, I love God. I go to church. I give money to help people in need. I don't cheat on my income taxes." These may be good things, but what is God's defini- tion? Jesus had already told His disciples very plainly:

> *"If you love me, you will obey what I command."*
> ∞ John 14:15

> *"Whoever has my commands and obeys them, he is the one who loves me."*
> ∞ John 14:21

This was pretty clear. Now He tells them what will be the result of their obedience:

> *"He who loves me will be loved by my Father, and I too will love him and* show *myself to him."*
>
> *Then Judas (not Judas Iscariot) said, "But, Lord, why do you intend to show yourself to us and not to the world?"*
>
> *Jesus replied, "If anyone loves me, he will obey my teaching. My Father will love him, and we will come to him and make our* home *with him. He who does not love me will not obey my teaching."*
>
> ∞ John 14:21–24, emphasis added

Let me explain the two words I emphasized in the last passage. When Jesus says that He will show Himself to the one who loves Him, the word *show* is the Greek word *emphanízō* Spiros Zodhiates, my Greek scholar of choice, tells us that this word means "to manifest oneself, meaning to let oneself be intimately known and understood."[3]

If we are sincere in our desire to experience intimacy with God, Jesus tells us how that can be accomplished: by *obeying* His teaching. If we obey Him, He knows that we truly love Him, and He will reveal Himself to us.

John's first epistle tells us, "This is love for God: to obey his commands. And his commands are not burdensome" (1 John 5:3). If God's commands are a burden to us, that is an indication of our intimacy level.

The second word I want to explain is the word *home*. Jesus said that for those who love Him, He and the Father will come and make Their home with him. The word *home* in the Greek is *moné*. It means "a mansion, habitation, abode."[4] It is the same word Jesus uses in John 14:2 when He says, "In my Father's house are many rooms [dwelling places]. . . . I am going there to prepare a place for you." This suggests an endearing fellowship among the Father, Jesus, and me. When we obey, They come and make Their "home" with us; They abide with us. It is the picture of a loving family dwelling together in harmony. We can experience that kind of love *when we obey.*

There is a cycle of increasing intimacy and communion with God that grows out of our obedience and leads to greater intimacy with God. The sequence is broken by disobedience. Memorizing Scripture has not removed sin or disobedience from my life, but it brings me back to God more quickly when I stray. When I am confronted throughout my day with God's holy words, I know I need to confess any sin right then. I don't want to have an entire day wasted, or even an hour. I don't want to stay away from God just because I have failed in some area. I want to run back without delay, restoring my fellowship with God and moving on.

For example, if I lose my temper and scream at my children while I'm driving them to school at 7:45 in the morning, I know I will drive home, sit at my desk, and stare out my window, not wanting to open my Bible. I can't review verses with a heart that is hardening. My day is a washout unless I get it straight with God. I can't memorize Scripture or even think about God if I know I'm off the path. I cannot go about my day under a cloud of false pretense. Instead of pouting about it or squandering my day, I come back to God, confessing, repenting, and seeking a fresh start—and it's still only 8:30 A.M. I haven't ruined my entire day, although I may have ruined my children's.

Am I saying that memorizing Scripture will make you want to obey God? Yes. Otherwise, you will quit memorizing. Remember, God told Joshua that if he meditated on God's Law day and night he would *be careful* to do all that is written in it. There are no guarantees that we will be faithful. Our only guarantee is that God will always be faithful. Let's follow God's recommendation and trust Him with the result.

Memorizing Scripture and constantly reviewing throughout the day will make you more sensitive to whether or not you are obeying. One afternoon while engaged in my favorite pastime—drinking coffee and reading the Word—I received a scolding from the Lord. I was reading in Psalm 50, and I paused after reading verses 16 and 17: "But to the wicked, God says: 'What right have you to recite my laws or take my covenant on your lips? You hate my instruction and cast my words behind you.'"

I read the verses again, slowly, and then I asked, "Lord, is this me?" I knew it was. I was harboring unforgiveness in my heart toward someone. In my mind, their offense was inexcusable. God's Word showed me that I had no right to go around reciting His Word and then not obey those same words. It was my offense that was inexcusable. God was not letting me get away with this transgression. The choice before me was either to surrender and ask for forgiveness or to put God's Word away. I chose to obey. My heart has become tender toward pleasing God and not violating the truths I have given my life to.

What about the charge that knowledge only puffs up and inflates the ego? I have heard that one a few dozen times. Actually, it is only knowledge without obedience that makes one prideful. True experiential knowledge will make you humble. When Isaiah saw a vision of God seated on His throne, high and exalted, he saw himself for what he really was, unworthy and unclean (Isaiah 6:1–5). When the apostle Peter finally realized that Jesus was the Christ, he said, "Go away from me, Lord; I am a sinful man!" (Luke 5:8). As we submit to God in obedience to His Word, we will keep a right perspective of who we are.

Our actions will always follow our beliefs. We live out each day what we truly believe. This is where we witness the progression from knowledge to obedience. I've seen it time and time again.

As God's Word solidifies truth in our hearts and minds, the inevitable result is a change in lifestyle, a change that reflects God's values over our own. Obedience is the true test of genuine faith.

But there is something within us that resists obedience. Can you identify with the well-known hymn by Robert Robinson (1735–90), "Come, Thou Fount of Every Blessing"?

> Prone to wander, Lord, I feel it,
> Prone to leave the God I love;
> Here's my heart, Lord, take and seal it;
> Seal it for Thy courts above.

Robinson recognized his human frailties, his proclivity to stray from the truth. And he cited the root of his problem, his deceptive heart. Thus, he asked God to take his heart and seal it so that it would be useful for God's kingdom only. Did he mean to seal his heart so that nothing else could penetrate it, or was he asking God to put His insignia on it so that God claims it as belonging to Him? I don't know. I know that when we

7
Your Turn:
THESE THINGS ARE EXCELLENT AND PROFITABLE FOR EVERYONE
Titus 2–3

This summer I received a most encouraging letter. Here is an abbreviated version:

> Dear Janet,
>
> About three years ago I really began to have a desire to memorize Scripture. I had set monthly and yearly goals, albeit small ones, and set out to learn verses at random. Though God blessed me in pressing some special verses on my heart, I wasn't satisfied with my attempts at hiding His Word in my heart. Time passed, and this spring you came to speak to the ladies at our church. With eagerness I attended. Your love for Christ and His Word radiated from you. You weren't proud or legalistic. You were just in love with God and enthusiastic

to encourage others to get to know God.

Here sits an inspired listener. I am so excited about God and His Word. He has enabled me to memorize 2 Peter and the first chapter of Colossians. As far as memorizing large chunks of the Bible, I won't advocate that everyone should, but I wouldn't give anything for how God has blessed me through my time in memorizing His truths.

Rather than worrying or speculating about some gossip I may have heard, I review Scripture. When my quiet husband enjoys silence on a car ride, I enjoy reviewing Scripture. When I wake up and can't sleep, I go over those verses again. As God provides opportunities, I share with others how exciting it's been to get to know Him.

God's Word must permeate every aspect of our lives. God can, indeed will, change our lives as we get to know Him. Sometimes I cry when I realize how precious God has been to me. What a joy that He allows us to get just a glimpse of who He is. Janet, thank you for pointing me in the right direction. God has used your willingness to share to bring me to new levels of knowing God. May God bless your ministry and lead many others to desire and to discipline themselves to know Him.

In Christ, Cindy

I wanted to share this letter with you, for just as God used me to inspire her, so I believe her testimony will inspire you. In a few months' time, she has memorized one book and started another, but her obvious joy and excitement is not in the accomplishment but in the resulting changes in her relationship with God, reaching new levels of knowing Him. As she closes her letter, she expresses hope that many others will desire and discipline themselves to know God. I was struck by her perception of what it takes—*desire* and *discipline*. Scripture memory cannot be accomplished without both. Many people have a desire but no discipline; some would discipline themselves if only they had the desire.

Memorizing Scripture can be compared to a regimen of taking a daily walk. It doesn't require great athletic ability or skill to walk around your neighborhood or on a walking track. In fact, it doesn't call for any athletic ability at all. It is not difficult, complicated, or expensive. So why are we impressed with the person who walks three miles a day? We could all do it if we chose to. Isn't that the answer? We admire them because they *choose* to exercise. We highly regard those individuals who choose to discipline themselves for a desired result, in this case, good health.

A year ago I was speaking at a conference in New Mexico, reciting 1 Peter. The next morning at breakfast, a woman sitting at my table began our conversation with "I'll bet you made straight A's in school." I shook my head and said, "No, I never did." My answer surprised her, because she assumed that what I had accomplished was reserved for brilliant people because it would come easily to them. She had already dismissed any notion of memorizing Scripture herself because she thought she wouldn't qualify. I shared my testimony with her and my reason for memorizing. It was not to conquer large passages but rather to develop and maintain a close walk with God. When we parted, a new challenge was before her. She too could do this if she had the desire and the discipline.

Several related principles are in place here:

∞ Our lives are a compilation of the choices we make.

∞ We reap what we sow.

∞ We will become what we are becoming.

If it is your goal to be a woman who knows God intimately and walks closely with Him, this will not happen overnight but only through consistent, deliberate choices you make on a daily basis. You will never become what you are not first in the *process* of becoming.

As we go through this chapter, may your prayer be: "O God, give me a desire so strong that I will choose to discipline myself."

Now we are ready for chapters 2 and 3 of Titus. I'll walk you through the first ten days.

Day One

:1 YOU MUST TEACH
WHAT IS IN ACCORD WITH SOUND DOCTRINE.

∞ Begin with verse 1. It's so short; you should have it down before you get out of the shower.

∞ Think about what the verse is saying, who said it, and to whom.

∞ Ask yourself, *What is sound doctrine? What is not sound doctrine?*

∞ Review and meditate on each word. Is this verse also applicable to mothers teaching their children?

∽ Make this verse a prayer to God that you will teach what is in accord with sound doctrine.

∽ Reflect on the word *must.* What if *Titus* does not teach what is in accord with sound doctrine? What if *you* do not?

∽ Ask God to teach you sound doctrine through your time in the book of Titus.

∽ Carry these words with you throughout the day, putting them into practice.

∽ Review periodically while doing chores, driving, or waiting.

∽ Come back to these words before bedtime. Have them solidified in your mind.

Day Two

:2 TEACH THE OLDER MEN TO BE TEMPERATE, WORTHY OF RESPECT, SELF-CONTROLLED, AND SOUND IN FAITH, IN LOVE AND IN ENDURANCE.

∽ When your alarm goes off, give your first thoughts to yesterday's verse. Have you got it?

∽ Today's verse is longer, so take it phrase by phrase.

∽ Work on it while you are getting dressed, making coffee, and eating breakfast.

∽ Ask yourself questions. *Who is Titus supposed to be teaching? What is he to teach them?*

∞ Why do older men need these qualities? Think about their roles in society and in a church.

∞ Keep saying this verse over and over.

∞ Define the words that describe what the older man should be.

∞ Review while dusting, folding laundry, or sweeping.

∞ Take your spiral book with you in the car so that you can maximize your time.

∞ Say verses 1 and 2 together. It may take fifteen or twenty times to remember these verses.

∞ Don't forget to review before you go to bed.

Day Three

:3 LIKEWISE, TEACH THE OLDER WOMEN
TO BE REVERENT IN THE WAY THEY LIVE,
NOT TO BE SLANDERERS OR ADDICTED TO MUCH WINE,
BUT TO TEACH WHAT IS GOOD.

∞ When you awaken, review your first two verses.

∞ Move on to today's verse. Take it phrase by phrase, or line by line.

∞ Who is this verse about? If you are not an older woman now, you will be one day.

∞ Think about the way women should behave, and why. What should they not do?

❧ Make this verse a plea to God for yourself and others you know.

❧ Think and meditate on God's reasons behind this instruction to Titus.

❧ Review all three of your verses while you're busy about your day.

❧ Keep your spiral cards on the kitchen counter while you cook dinner or do dishes.

❧ Review some more during the evening hours and before you go to bed.

Day Four

:4 THEN THEY CAN TRAIN THE YOUNGER WOMEN
TO LOVE THEIR HUSBANDS AND CHILDREN,

❧ Get out of bed thinking about God and His invaluable Word. Review your three verses.

❧ Tackle today's verse, another short one. What is God saying?

❧ Notice the connection to yesterday's verse. Today we get the reason behind verse 3.

❧ We hear a lot of talk these days about mentoring. This is where it comes from: Titus.

❧ Keep saying all four verses over and over as you reflect on their meaning.

❧ Are you the younger woman? What are you to be doing? Ask God to enable you.

∽ These four verses will take less than thirty seconds to review. Find pockets of time to do so.

∽ Are you waiting in the car pool line at school? Take this time to go over your verses.

∽ Come back to these words before you retire for the night. Drift off to sleep thinking and praying.

Day Five

:5 TO BE SELF-CONTROLLED AND PURE, TO BE BUSY AT HOME, TO BE KIND, AND TO BE SUBJECT TO THEIR HUSBANDS, SO THAT NO ONE WILL MALIGN THE WORD OF GOD.

∽ Take the first thirty seconds of your day to review your progress. Then go on to verse 5.

∽ Today's verse is so very practical. Proceed slowly and thoroughly. You don't want to miss a word.

∽ Think about the what, why, and how in these instructions.

∽ Concentrate on the words, going over them again and again.

∽ Review as you drive your children to school, or as you drive to work, or wherever you go.

∽ What does this verse say will happen if young women don't do these things? Think about it.

∽ Share these words with a friend who also needs that encouragement.

∽ Keep saying this verse out loud, speaking words of exhortation to yourself.

∽ Make these words a prayer to God to transform you into His ideal woman. Then trust Him to do it.

∽ Come back often to today's verse, working to implant it into your memory for future use.

∽ Remember to review before you go to bed. This will guard your thought life.

Day Six

:6 SIMILARLY,
ENCOURAGE THE YOUNG MEN TO BE SELF-CONTROLLED.

∽ A new day and a new verse. Start with the previous five and then move on to verse 6.

∽ Recite today's verse at least ten times while getting ready for the day.

∽ Keep the TV off and review verses instead.

∽ Are you seeing any similarities in Paul's instructions to the different people? What and why?

∽ Review all six verses while you walk the dog, or walk yourself, or push the baby stroller.

∽ Think about what the body of Christ would be like if we all obeyed these instructions.

∽ Don't forget to review Psalm 1 on your designated day, as well as Titus 1.

∽ Keep your mind and heart surrendered to God's thoughts. Is He teaching you something?

∽ Come back at lunch to feast on God's Word. Take every thought captive.

∽ Mundane chores and errands can become joyful when you include Scripture review.

∽ Conclude your day by rehearsing what God is teaching you in His Word.

Day Seven

:7 IN EVERYTHING SET THEM AN EXAMPLE
BY DOING WHAT IS GOOD.
IN YOUR TEACHING SHOW INTEGRITY, SERIOUSNESS

∽ Discipline yourself to give your first thoughts to God.

∽ Review what you've learned so far. See if you can do it all in the shower without looking. Then jump into verse 7. Take it slowly and carefully.

∽ Today's verse includes when and who and how and what. Look for these. They're all important.

∽ Keep reviewing throughout the day. Learn to recite Scripture while doing other things.

∽ You're up to about forty-five seconds. Try to squeeze in several review times.

∽ Say the words out loud so that you can hear them. This will aid the learning process.

∽ End your day with God's Word. Don't forget the blessing is in meditating day and night.

Day Eight

:8 AND SOUNDNESS OF SPEECH THAT CANNOT BE
   CONDEMNED,
SO THAT THOSE WHO OPPOSE YOU MAY BE ASHAMED
BECAUSE THEY HAVE NOTHING BAD TO SAY ABOUT US.

∽ Wake up to a new day eager for more of God's truth. Go over your seven verses.

∽ Can you see God's character in the things He commands for us?

∽ Today's verse gives a why for the previous verse. Our reputation depends on our obedience.

∽ But how can we obey if we don't know? That's why we're learning God's instructions.

∽ Learn God's Word so that those who oppose you will have nothing bad to say.

∽ Let this verse be a prayer to God to build in you an impeccable character and a sterling reputation so that God will be exalted by your life. He wants to honor that kind of prayer.

∽ Say your verses over and over.

∽ Find a kindred spirit to share what God is teaching you.

∾ Give God your full attention at day's end.
Thank Him that His Word shall not return void.

Day Nine

:9 TEACH SLAVES TO BE SUBJECT TO THEIR MASTERS
   IN EVERYTHING,
TO TRY TO PLEASE THEM,
NOT TO TALK BACK TO THEM,

∾ Another day to learn something else. Start by reviewing your eight previous verses.

∾ Add today's verse, line by line. You are establishing such good habits. Congratulate yourself.

∾ Though we do not live in a society with slaves, how else can this verse apply?

∾ Ask God for insights as you go over and over these words.

∾ Come back throughout your day. Take one-minute breaks for God's Word.

∾ Tell your kids what you're learning. They need it, too.

∾ Keep your spiral with you wherever you go. You never know when you'll have a spare moment.

∾ Folding laundry and putting fresh sheets on beds are perfect times for review.

∽ Sweeping and vacuuming are two chores made easier when your mind is somewhere else.

∽ Raking leaves goes much quicker if you review passages at the same time.

∽ Always come back to God's Word before bed. If you're too exhausted, just read it.

Day Ten

:10 AND NOT TO STEAL FROM THEM,
BUT TO SHOW THAT THEY CAN BE FULLY TRUSTED,
SO THAT IN EVERY WAY
THEY WILL MAKE THE TEACHING ABOUT GOD OUR SAVIOR
ATTRACTIVE.

∽ Begin your day with God. Don't miss a single day. Review while you do other things.

∽ Add your new verse. You are up to one-minute review time for chapter 2.

∽ Review while you put on makeup and fix your hair.

∽ Look at your verses over breakfast and while making school lunches.

∽ Ask questions that pertain to this verse. The life of an obedient and trusted slave would attract others to the Savior. Can this apply to us as well?

∽ Pray about your lifestyle. Ask God to make you an attractive witness for Him.

℮ Find one-minute pockets in your day to go over these ten verses.

℮ Call a friend and tell her what God is doing in your life. She'll be so blessed.

℮ Recite your verses in the car, in a traffic jam. Turn off the radio and listen to God instead.

℮ Repeat the ten verses when you crawl into bed after a full day.

I'm leaving you on your own for the next twenty days. You know what to do. Press on. The reward is in the process, not the finish line. Train yourself to ask such questions as, Who? What? Where? When? Why? How? There's so much to learn. Look for some great doctrines coming up in this chapter and the next one. Take a break after chapter 2 if you need one. Otherwise, keep going. God is with you, and He is delighted in you.

Day Eleven
:11 FOR THE GRACE OF GOD THAT BRINGS SALVATION HAS APPEARED TO ALL MEN.

Day Twelve
:12 IT TEACHES US TO SAY "NO"
TO UNGODLINESS AND WORLDLY PASSIONS,
AND TO LIVE SELF-CONTROLLED, UPRIGHT AND GODLY LIVES
IN THIS PRESENT AGE,

Day Thirteen

:13 WHILE WE WAIT FOR THE BLESSED HOPE—
THE GLORIOUS APPEARING
OF OUR GREAT GOD AND SAVIOR, JESUS CHRIST,

Day Fourteen

:14 WHO GAVE HIMSELF FOR US
TO REDEEM US FROM ALL WICKEDNESS
AND TO PURIFY FOR HIMSELF
A PEOPLE THAT ARE HIS VERY OWN,
EAGER TO DO WHAT IS GOOD.

Day Fifteen

:15 THESE, THEN, ARE THE THINGS YOU SHOULD TEACH.
ENCOURAGE AND REBUKE WITH ALL AUTHORITY.
DO NOT LET ANYONE DESPISE YOU.

Day Sixteen

3:1 REMIND THE PEOPLE
TO BE SUBJECT TO RULERS AND AUTHORITIES,
TO BE OBEDIENT,
TO BE READY TO DO WHATEVER IS GOOD,

Day Seventeen

:2 TO SLANDER NO ONE,
TO BE PEACEABLE AND CONSIDERATE,
AND TO SHOW TRUE HUMILITY TOWARD ALL MEN.

Day Eighteen

:3 AT ONE TIME WE TOO WERE FOOLISH, DISOBEDIENT,
DECEIVED AND ENSLAVED BY ALL KINDS OF PASSIONS
    AND PLEASURES.
WE LIVED IN MALICE AND ENVY,
BEING HATED AND HATING ONE ANOTHER.

Day Nineteen

:4 BUT WHEN THE KINDNESS AND LOVE
OF GOD OUR SAVIOR APPEARED,

Day Twenty

:5 HE SAVED US,
NOT BECAUSE OF RIGHTEOUS THINGS WE HAD DONE,
BUT BECAUSE OF HIS MERCY.
HE SAVED US THROUGH THE WASHING OF REBIRTH
AND RENEWAL BY THE HOLY SPIRIT,

Day Twenty-One

:6 WHOM HE POURED OUT ON US GENEROUSLY
THROUGH JESUS CHRIST OUR SAVIOR,

Day Twenty-Two

:7 SO THAT, HAVING BEEN JUSTIFIED BY HIS GRACE,
WE MIGHT BECOME HEIRS
HAVING THE HOPE OF ETERNAL LIFE.

Day Twenty-Three

:8 THIS IS A TRUSTWORTHY SAYING.
AND I WANT YOU TO STRESS THESE THINGS,
SO THAT THOSE WHO HAVE TRUSTED IN GOD
MAY BE CAREFUL TO DEVOTE THEMSELVES TO DOING
  WHAT IS GOOD.
THESE THINGS ARE EXCELLENT AND PROFITABLE FOR
  EVERYONE.

Day Twenty-Four

:9 BUT AVOID FOOLISH CONTROVERSIES AND GENEALOGIES
AND ARGUMENTS AND QUARRELS ABOUT THE LAW,
BECAUSE THESE ARE UNPROFITABLE AND USELESS.

Day Twenty-Five

:10 WARN A DIVISIVE PERSON ONCE,
AND THEN WARN HIM A SECOND TIME.
AFTER THAT, HAVE NOTHING TO DO WITH HIM.

Day Twenty-Six

:11 YOU MAY BE SURE THAT SUCH A MAN
IS WARPED AND SINFUL;
HE IS SELF-CONDEMNED.

Day Twenty-Seven

:12 AS SOON AS I SEND ARTEMAS OR TYCHICUS TO YOU,
DO YOUR BEST TO COME TO ME AT NICOPOLIS,
BECAUSE I HAVE DECIDED TO WINTER THERE.

Day Twenty-Eight

:13 Do EVERYTHING YOU CAN TO HELP ZENAS THE LAWYER
AND APOLLOS ON THEIR WAY
AND SEE THAT THEY HAVE EVERYTHING THEY NEED.

Day Twenty-Nine

:14 OUR PEOPLE MUST LEARN
TO DEVOTE THEMSELVES TO DOING WHAT IS GOOD,
IN ORDER THAT THEY MAY PROVIDE FOR DAILY NECESSITIES
AND NOT LIVE UNPRODUCTIVE LIVES.

Day Thirty

:15 EVERYONE WITH ME SENDS YOU GREETINGS.
GREET THOSE WHO LOVE US IN THE FAITH.
GRACE BE WITH YOU ALL.

Hurray! You've crossed the finish line. Well done!
Enjoy the satisfaction of a goal achieved. It wasn't all
that difficult, was it? You plodded along, slow and
steady, and nourished your soul along the way. You
chose God as your companion, and He was with you
and in you.

Now that you know the words in your head, keep
praying that God will take these truths and transcribe
them onto your heart so that you will live like a person
who is the recipient of God's kindness and mercy and is
waiting for the blessed hope, the appearing of your
great God and Savior.

So where do you go from here? First, take the next
few days, even up to a week, to review the whole book
of Titus each day. It will take six to seven minutes for all
three chapters. Recite Titus, in its entirety, in the morn-

ing, at night, and whenever you can fit it in during the day. Ask your husband or a friend to listen while you go through it. This will help to solidify the text in your mind and give you confidence that you know it.

After that, review Titus on your designated day, once a week. This will keep you from losing it. After a year, you will have reviewed it an additional fifty-two times. This is important in order to move it from short-term memory to long-term memory. By having it accessible in long-term memory, you'll be amazed at how God will bring portions of it to your mind right when you need it, for yourself or for someone else. Don't keep it to yourself. It's yours to share.

One of the most common objections to memorizing Scripture is, "Eventually I forget what I've memorized." This is legitimate. If we do not constantly review, we will forget the vast majority of what we memorize. Two important aspects of Scripture memory already mentioned in this book bear repeating here:

1. The process itself will profoundly impact your life. If the goal of memorizing is to know God and keep Him in your mind and heart throughout the day, and if it is the process that keeps you meditating day and night on God and His thoughts, then all is not lost if you can't remember it weeks later. If memorizing a verse gives you courage to face the day and strength to keep walking with God in the midst of adversity, what does it matter if you forget the exact words two months from now? The goal has been met.

2. The discipline of reviewing has innumerable benefits for the future. Adding to your warehouse of

biblical knowledge will make those truths available to you whenever you need them. This stored knowledge also serves as a filter through which to process new information the world throws at you, validating some messages and rejecting other, incompatible messages. The passages of Scripture you store in your memory will be building blocks added to the foundation of your relationship with God that will continue to transform your thinking about God and yourself.

I could summarize these two points by saying that if you continue to review a book after you've learned it, you'll have added benefits; but even if you never, ever review it again, you still will have experienced something invaluable—time spent focused on God and His Word.

So what's next? That's up to you. You may want to go to something shorter, such as a psalm or a proverb, or a short passage. Write out the text in the same spiral cardholder; you should have room left. I usually put a paper clip at the beginning of a new project so that I can find it more quickly. Begin whenever you're ready, but don't wait too long. You have worked diligently to establish a habit. If you leave it, you may have difficulty getting back on track.

Let me tell you about a fourth grade class at Pinecastle Christian Academy in Orlando, Florida. These students took on a memorization project, the book of James. This is how it worked. There are 108 verses in James and thirty-six weeks of school, which breaks down to three verses per week. The class spent a few minutes each day learning their new verses and reviewing the old ones.

By the end of the school year, every one of these children could recite the entire book of James, and they did so in an evening church service in front of their proud parents and the congregation. What a witness! These nine- and ten-year-olds accomplished much more than memory work. They had God's Word implanted in their hearts and lives. They could have memorized 108 separate, unrelated verses, but a wise teacher saw the value of learning an entire book. I was so impressed to hear about this, and I knew you would be, too.

Many people have asked me if I recommend listening to the Bible on tape. I recommend anything that works for you. Personally, it doesn't seem to help me. I think it's because I need to hear myself saying the words. Experiment with it yourself and see if it works for you. I don't claim to have the best method. I developed a system that works for me. Create your own or adapt mine to fit your lifestyle. At this point in my life, I take many trips, and driving to the airport is ninety miles one way. I use that time in the car to review my long books, such as Hebrews and Revelation. When I'm not traveling, I break the books down into chapters because it can be difficult to squeeze in forty-five minutes or more for review.

Several years ago, when we were still living in Dallas, we got a phone call in the middle of the night. It was the police, saying that Ethan's office had been broken into and that he needed to come down right away and identify what was missing. He returned home an hour later with good and bad news. The good news was that they had only stolen his computer and printer. There was no vandalism or mess to clean up. The loss would be covered by insurance.

Then the bad news. "I have not backed up my computer in six weeks." What did that mean? All the data he'd put into the computer in the previous six weeks was not stored on a backup diskette. The conference manual he'd been working on for weeks was now lost; he'd have to start over. This was a painful lesson for Ethan, one he's never forgotten: If something is important and you don't want to lose it, make sure you have backup copies of the information.

Have you ever considered that memorizing Scripture has a built-in security system? They can steal your computer and your Bible, but they can't steal what you've stored in your memory. No one can take that from you!

> *The mouth of the righteous man utters wisdom,*
> *and his tongue speaks what is just.*
> *The law of his God is in his heart;*
> *his feet do not slip.*
> ∽ Psalm 37:30–31

8

Benefit #3:

BLESSED IS THE MAN
WHO TRUSTS IN THE LORD

As I continued to immerse myself in God's Word, the bond between me and my heavenly Father grew deeper than I would ever have imagined. Desiring to please Him kept me on the path of obedience, which in turn brought me nearer to His heart. My time in His Word each day was so precious and so sweet, and the Scriptures I had memorized were a constant affirmation as I reviewed one book every day throughout the day.

A new year had just arrived, and I was looking for a fresh opportunity. I wanted to memorize something I was not familiar with, so I decided to take on the book of Hebrews. It is a unique book that connects the Old Testament temple, sacrifices, and priests with their fulfillment in Jesus Christ. I wanted so much to know and understand these truths fully. If I took one chapter a month, I could finish in a year. No, there are thirteen chapters! OK, I'll squeeze one in somewhere. To add to the challenge, I decided to study and teach the book of Hebrews at the same time. I began on January 1, eager and ready to learn.

The message of Hebrews is rich, elevating Jesus and the role He came to fulfill.

> ∞ He was much superior to the angels.

> ∞ He was worthy of greater honor than Moses.

> ∞ He was a merciful and faithful High Priest.

> ∞ He was a better sacrifice than bulls and goats.

I was in continual awe of my Savior and all He had done for me. Little did I know that God was preparing me for my life's greatest sorrow.

My father, who had had four heart attacks and cancer, died on July 7. We had known for months that he was dying, and I had made two trips to my parents' home in Orlando to plead with him to consider Jesus. Everyone I could possibly think of was praying for my dad, including our two children, ages eight and eleven at the time. But he did not believe that Jesus was the only way to God, and no amount of convincing would change his heart. And so he died—without hope and without Christ.

When the call came that day, we huddled together as a family. My children looked at me with inconsolable faces and said, "What are we going to do?" I remember the words that came out of my mouth: "We're going to trust God. He will get us through this."

An hour later my mother phoned to ask if I would speak at the funeral. I was frozen by her question. It's not that I was unwilling, but what would I say? What *could* I say? There was no bright side to this tragedy, no happy ending, no future reunion. It was over! I couldn't get up there and quote a few Bible verses and pretend everything was all right. *O God, I can't do this!* But I knew I had to. My mother had just lost a husband of forty-five years. My children had lost their "Pop." There would be other family members there as well as my father's co-workers and golfing buddies. So I would trust God, and He would be with me.

The most difficult assignment of my life had just been handed to me. I called my closest friends to pray for me, hold me up, and protect me from despair. My most pressing need was for God's help in writing and delivering a tribute to my father.

We got our things together and packed the car. An hour before we left, my friend Melissa dropped by and said, "I thought this might be helpful," as she handed me Dennis Rainey's book, *The Tribute.* There is no doubt it was the hand of God.

During the twelve-hour drive, I read the book, much of the time by flashlight, and wrote a tribute to my father. From a human perspective, I was fragile and vulnerable, but in the truest sense, God was my refuge and strength. He was the unwavering strength that gave me the courage to face the task, even though my heart was breaking. I clung to His words as if they were my very life. And when the time came for me to speak, "God's grace and peace were *mine* in abundance."

When I returned home to Hattiesburg, my friends showered me with love and support. God was so near. His Word had been tested and was standing firm. The truths of Hebrews were ever present. After spending months studying and meditating on all that Jesus did to give us access to the Holy of Holies, the very throne room of God, I had no reason to stand afar in the outer court. I came boldly and often to His throne of grace, and He was always there.

Several weeks later, on a Sunday night in church, we had been singing and praising God when an evangelist got up to speak. He said, "Tonight, I am going to tell you the truth about hell." I was caught totally off guard. Sitting in the second pew, I felt conspicuous and trapped. As I moved closer to Ethan, he put his arm around me, both of us dreading what was coming. By the end of the service, I was distraught and beaten down. We made a beeline for the exit and drove home in silence.

The next morning during my prayer time, I cried out in desperation. "God, I can't cry myself to sleep every night because my father is in a place of torment. I know too much to pretend it isn't true, and I don't know how to live with this." And, momentarily, in my heart, I doubted that even God's Word had an answer for this.

Later on that day, while folding laundry, I was reviewing the book of Philippians from memory, which I did every Monday. When I got to the part in chapter 3 that says, "I want to know Christ and the power of his resurrection and the fellowship of sharing in his sufferings," God interrupted me and said, "There's your answer! Now you know the suffering of My Son. Now you know the pain caused by one you love who rejects the truth . . . the pain caused by sin . . . the pain caused by pride and indifference. Do you really want to know Christ and the fellowship of sharing in His suffering . . . or are these just words on a page?"

Now *God* was asking the questions. I felt as though I were suspended in midair and not coming down until I gave Him an answer. I said, "Yes, Lord, I want to know Christ. I want You to use the pain in my heart to draw me closer to my Savior, a Man of Sorrows and acquainted with grief." God's Word was there for me once again. It truly is everything I need for life and godliness.

I share this pain with you because suffering is universal, and Christians are by no means exempt from it. We carry emotional scars with us that have come about through ended relationships, financial reversals, tragedies and betrayals, serious or chronic illnesses, and private wounds that cannot be shared with anyone. We will all be tested through trials. Peter tells us it's God's way of proving that our faith is genuine. When things don't go our way, will we still believe? Will we still obey? Will we continue to trust God even if He says no to our prayers—or doesn't answer at all?

Every life is sprinkled with adversity, and no family goes untouched. Heartache and struggle are persistent guests in every home. When hardship comes knocking at your door, how will you deal with it? Will you retreat into depression? Will you lash out at your spouse? At your kids? At God? What will you tell your children when life is cruel and unfair? When God could have intervened but didn't? They are learning to deal with life's disappointments by watching you. If you don't trust God, will they?

God intended His Word to be our anchor in the storms of life. Within the pages of His Book, He builds, precept upon precept, a picture of the One we can trust. He is a righteous God, perfect and holy in all His ways. He is the God who knows all things, who sees the beginning and the end and whatever lies in between. He has the power and authority to orchestrate all events, working out everything in conformity with the purpose of His will. He is the ultimate Ruler over all and sovereign in the affairs of men and nations.

Do I understand all of this? No, but I accept it, nonetheless. And most beneficial from my human perspective, He is a Father who cares. He is the One I belong to, the One who redeemed me with a price. He is the Shepherd willing to leave the other ninety-nine sheep in order to bring back the one gone astray. He longs to be gracious to me and waits on high to have compassion on me. His thoughts of me are too numerous to be counted, and His plans for me are sifted through loving hands. This is the God I have read about and have come to know, and so I trust Him.

This trust is no doubt the by-product of God's Word, which has been sown in my life. My heartache over my father's lost condition is still with me, and I can only imagine where I would be if God's Word were not my constant source of strength. I would either be in denial or in despair. My father's situation is beyond my human capacity to deal with or resolve, either emotionally or providentially. All I know is that I have left the matter with God and can trust Him. He doesn't have to report to me. He owes me no explanation. His Word says that one day all tears and sorrow will cease. This promise is more enduring than my pain. I choose to believe it, and until then I'll keep trusting Him to be my refuge from a situation I cannot change.

Sometimes uncertainty is more unsettling than adversity. There are so many unknown variables in raising a family. Children are complex beings; no two are alike. Not all parenting guidelines are one-solution-fits-all, but neither is parenting arbitrary. Every conscientious mother wrestles with decisions affecting her children. Many choices are not black and white; there is a lot of gray. We live in uncertain times. We fear we'll take the wrong path, but ambivalence makes us crazy. So where do we go; where do we turn?

It would be simplistic to reply that the Bible holds all the answers to life's questions. Or *would* it? The Bible is complete in that it reveals all that God intended for us to know about Him; and in knowing Him we will have everything we need for life and godliness. But the Bible has not answered every single question, nor has it addressed all situations we will encounter. You cannot open the Bible and point to a specific verse every time you face a decision. You can seek God with all your heart and obey Him faithfully, and yet there will still be times when you don't have a clue as to what to do, which road to take, or when it's time to call it quits.

It would be inconsistent with God's nature to say that He "forgot" to include a few things, so we can assume that whatever he left out of his word was intentional. God never planned to settle all mysteries for us or to explain all His reasons. He has told us what we need to know, and He wants us to trust Him with the rest. "Trust in the LORD with all your heart and lean not on your own understanding; in all your ways acknowledge him, and he will make your paths straight" (Proverbs 3:5–6). God appeals to us to trust Him. Trusting Him is an indispensable part of the Christian life; we cannot grow as believers without it. Our human tendency is to trust in ourselves, but Proverbs warns us, "He who trusts in his own heart is a fool" (Proverbs 28:26 NASB).

What does it *really* mean to trust God, and how can we learn to trust Him? Trust is not a difficult concept to understand; the challenge is living it out day-to-day. *The Merriam-Webster Dictionary, Home and Office Edition* (1998) defines the noun as "assured reliance on the character, strength or truth of someone or something"; the verb form is "to place confidence." These definitions clearly describe our trust in God. Because we are sure of His character, strength, and truthfulness, we place our confidence in Him; we depend on Him. Likewise, our trust in God is dependent on our trust in His Word, for that is where we learn about His character, strength, and truthfulness.

God reveals in His Word:

∞ *His character:* He is holy and good and just. He is loving and merciful.

∞ *His strength:* He is all-powerful, present everywhere, knowing all things, and unchanging.

∞ *His truthfulness:* He will not lie, deceive, or misrepresent.

This is the God we can know and trust. Just as there is a definite link between knowing God and knowing His Word, so there is an inseparable connection between knowing God's Word and trusting Him. As God communicates truth in His Word, I have something to hold on to and to put my trust in. It's a progressive learning experience—the more I trust God for things He *has* made known in His Word, the more I am able to trust Him for things He has *not* made known.

A few years ago, my daughter, age thirteen at the time, came home from church camp with a fever of

105.8 degrees. After a doctor's visit and some medication, the fever came down, but days later it was back up. I phoned our doctor and asked him bluntly if a child could die from such a high fever. His response was noncommittal.

After hanging up, I realized that he wasn't holding back on giving me assurance; he *couldn't* give me assurance because he hadn't yet determined what was wrong with Natalie. As I sat by her bed waiting for the fever to come down, my thoughts turned to Psalm 139:16: "All the days ordained for me were written in your book before one of them came to be." Did I trust this verse? Absolutely. Although it was not the answer to my question, it gave me what I needed to trust God. It reassured me that Natalie's life was in God's hands. She couldn't die without God's permission; neither could she stay alive longer than God had decreed. This verse and many others carried me through the next few weeks of tests, and more tests, and finally through the surgery she needed.

On their final night together, Jesus told His disciples, "The Counselor, the Holy Spirit, whom the Father will send in my name, will teach you all things and will remind you of everything I have said to you" (John 14:26). This is true for us as well; the Holy Spirit is our resident Teacher, and He continually reminds us of the things God has said. Countless times, in the precise moment I have needed it, the Holy Spirit has brought to my mind something specific I have memorized. He has used those same words to teach me and direct me, to rebuke me and turn me around. His words have shed light on my situation and have given me God's perspective. It stands to reason that if I didn't have any Scriptures stored up, He couldn't *remind* me of them.

In that sense, memorizing Scripture gives the Holy Spirit something to work with. Once again, I don't want to imply that all Scripture has to be memorized to be useful. I'm just saying that by memorizing it, we place it in our minds so that the Holy Spirit can bring it back to us at an opportune time. For me, trust is one of those areas in which I need continual reminders. When I start to worry about things, He brings many different verses to mind. I now have a reservoir of verses to draw from. Each verse has its own slant, but all ask the question, " Will you trust God in this?"

Trusting . . . it's a similar concept to faith. Whereas the word *faith* is used primarily in the New Testament, *trust* is used primarily in the Old Testament. Both terms describe confidence and reliance on God, and both are part of our calling as Christians. Not surprisingly, both are affected by knowing God's Word. Paul tells us in Romans that "faith comes by hearing, and hearing by the word of God" (Romans 10:17 NKJV). King David says in Psalm 56, "In God, whose word I praise, in God I trust" (Psalm 56:4).

At the beginning of last summer, I was going through a time of feeling frustrated about a situation I had turned over to God months before but was not seeing any action on. I kept waiting and waiting and wondering why God was not doing anything about it. I was looking for a chapter or passage to memorize that would give me patience. Instead, God led me to what I really needed to do—trust Him. The Scripture passage was Isaiah 55. Included in this chapter are these words:

> *"For my thoughts are not your thoughts,*
> *neither are your ways my ways,"*

> *declares the LORD.*
> *"As the heavens are higher than the earth,*
> *so are my ways higher than your ways*
> *and my thoughts than your thoughts."*
> ∾ Isaiah 55:8–9

I had heard these verses many times before, but in memorizing them, saying them over and over, I had a chance to meditate on them, to ponder their depth, and come to a fuller understanding. God was saying to me, "Don't put Me on your level! My thoughts and ways are so much grander than yours, you can't even fathom the distance." That was a humbling thought, and humbled I was.

As a parent, have you ever made a promise to your children that you couldn't keep? Sure; we all have. Perhaps new information made us change our minds, or circumstances came up beyond our control, or somehow we just weren't able to come through. Do we sometimes put God on the level of an imperfect parent bound by circumstances or incomplete knowledge? Are we guilty of giving Him human attributes? The reason God had not answered my plea was not because He was tired or unconcerned or too busy. He didn't have a conflict of interest or a schedule jam. He was not still contemplating what He should do. Honestly, I don't know why God put my request on hold; He didn't tell me. What He told me was, "My way is best; trust Me." Did it take memorizing an entire chapter to get that message? For me, yes. He'd probably been trying to tell me for months, but either I wasn't listening or I was too bullheaded to hear.

The following verses about God's ways and thoughts relate to this point.

"As the rain and the snow
come down from heaven
and do not return to it
without watering the earth
and making it bud and flourish,
so that it yields seed for the sower and bread for the eater,
so is my word that goes out from my mouth:
It will not return to me empty,
but will accomplish what I desire
and achieve the purpose for which I sent it."
    ∞ Isaiah 55:10–11

Although I have always loved these verses, I had never connected them to the two verses preceding them. But after saying the verses together some three hundred times, a light went on. Why is God's Word so adept at producing life and growth? *Because it contains God's thoughts and God's ways.* When we get into God's Word, it becomes our pipeline to God's way of thinking and doing things. As I stay in God's Word, abiding in God's Word, drinking in God's Word, letting it go deep, it will do its work in me, the work it was sent to do. *It will accomplish God's desire and achieve His purpose,* which is to cause growth in me by bringing my thoughts and my ways into alignment with His.

Memorizing Scripture is never unproductive time. It is an oasis for the mind and soul. I have learned so much and have enjoyed such deep communion with the Lord that I can never go back to just reading God's Word. As I memorize His Word, He patiently teaches me things I need to know so that I can trust Him more. Isaiah 55 is an awesome chapter, calling me to come and drink freely and reassuring me that God's Word will not return void. All that I have memorized keeps working in my life. Not one word is irrelevant or wasted.

The book of Proverbs contains this advice:

> *Pay attention and listen to the sayings of the wise;*
> *apply your heart to what I teach,*
> *for it is pleasing when you* keep them in your heart
> *and have all of them* ready on your lips.
> So that your trust may be in the LORD,
> *I teach you today, even you.*
> ∞ Proverbs 22:17–19, emphasis added

Can you see a link here between memorizing Scripture and trusting the Lord? When God's words are in your heart and on your lips, you will grow confident in those very words. You will depend on them for insight and inspiration. You will rely on them for courage and protection. "The LORD is my strength and shield; my heart trusts in him, and I am helped" (Psalm 28:7).

I am helped. That's my point here. I memorize Scripture because it's in my best interest. I can't make it on my own, and I know it. Life is too difficult, and there is too much uncertainty. My nature is to take the path of least resistance. I don't want a fight; I'd rather run and hide. My own resources are inadequate to carry me through the daily complexities of raising a family, not to mention life in general. My human judgment is impaired; my knowledge, insufficient; my discernment, flawed. Having acknowledged all that, I should think it would be easy to trust an all- knowing and perfectly

wise God, but because of my depraved nature, I need
help even with trusting.

> *"Blessed is the man who trusts in the LORD,*
> *whose confidence is in him.*
> *He will be like a tree planted by the water*
> *that sends out its roots by the stream.*
> *It does not fear when heat comes;*
> *its leaves are always green.*
> *It has no worries in a year of drought*
> *and never fails to bear fruit."*
> ∾ Jeremiah 17:7–8

Here is one more tree analogy. This tree, however,
though planted near the water, *sends out* its roots to get
that water. Similarly, though we may know that God's
Word is a source of life for us, we must go out and get
it. It's not enough to own a Bible; we must make the
effort to get into it and to know it and to drink from it
continually. In doing so, we'll not be afraid when the
heat is on, when the pressures of life threaten to scorch
us. Our growth will not be hindered; we'll stay alive
and fresh and green. We cannot escape times of
drought, but we don't have to be consumed with worry
in the midst of them. Our Father is taking care of us
and working in our lives to produce fruit even in the
toughest of times.

Psalm 121 is a favorite psalm of reassurance that I
have reviewed hundreds of times; it never grows old:

I lift up my eyes to the hills—
where does my help come from?
My help comes from the LORD,
the Maker of heaven and earth.

He will not let your foot slip—
he who watches over you will not slumber;
indeed, he who watches over Israel
will neither slumber nor sleep.

The LORD watches over you—
the LORD is your shade at your right hand;
the sun will not harm you by day,
nor the moon by night.

The LORD will keep you from all harm—
he will watch over your life;
the LORD will watch over your coming and going
both now and forevermore.

These are words of life to remind me that God is watching over me and that I can trust Him.

Are you having difficulty trusting God with some aspect of your life? Do you sometimes doubt His Word, mistrust His motives, or hold Him under suspicion? Do you long to trust Him more, to be able to say with Job, "Though he slay me, yet will I trust in him"? (Job 13:15 KJV). As a fellow struggler, I admit that I have often wrestled with the same doubts. Over the last ten years, I have grown tremendously in this area and have observed from my own experience that trusting God is a choice and can easily become a habit. The more you know God and His Word, the more you will see His impeccable character, and the more you will be able to trust that His decisions are right and His ways best. The choice becomes, "Will I take God at His Word?" The more you say yes to this question, the easier it will be the next time.

Find a passage to memorize in an area where you are wavering. Let God work His truth into your heart by giving Him the opportunity to display His trustworthiness showcased in the Bible. It's OK if it takes several months to finish. What could be more important? Each lesson learned will become a landmark in your journey with Christ. You'll not regret a single step.

The blessing of trust occurs not merely in the high and low points of life but also in the day-to-day grind, the daily tasks and chores, the hour-by-hour duties of keeping a household running and attending to the concerns of our families. The *world* cannot give us a guarantee that everything will work out for good to those who love God and are called according to His purpose. That is *God's* promise to fulfill, and His alone. We labor and toil now, not seeing the end, but trusting Him to be true to His Word. "Therefore, my beloved brethren, be steadfast, immovable, always abounding in the work of the Lord, knowing that your toil is not in vain in the Lord" (1 Corinthians 15:58 NASB).

None of us will see the fulfillment of God's plan on this side of eternity. We're called to walk by faith, not by sight. But we're not laboring alone; we have a great cloud of witnesses who went before us. The people in Hebrews 11 never saw the fulfillment of the promises made to Israel. We are told, "All these people were still living by faith when they died. They did not receive the things promised; they only saw them and welcomed them from a distance" (Hebrews 11:13).

I want my heart to be a "welcome center" for all the promises of God, even if I never see their fulfillment this side of heaven. And when hardship and uncertainty descend on my life, I want to be steadfast and persevering, clinging to His Word and trusting in His promises. God's Word in my heart and on my lips takes the focus off my circumstances and keeps the spotlight on my Redeemer, my Jehovah Shalom.

> *Thou wilt keep him in perfect peace, whose mind is stayed on thee: because he trusteth in thee.*
> ∞ Isaiah 26:3 KJV

> *"Trust in the Lord forever,*
> *for in God the Lord, we have an everlasting Rock."*
> ∞ Isaiah 26:4 NASB

9

Conclusion:

TRANSFORMED BY THE RENEWING OF YOUR MIND

*T*wenty-plus years ago, I had a very special friend who lived next door to me. One day, he came over and shared a motivational Scripture verse with me. We decided to memorize that verse together and have always reminded each other of its claim on our lives. Eventually, I married that friend, and we made it our life verse, inscribing the reference numbers onto our wedding bands. This is what the verse and the surrounding text say (typeset as poetry):

> *For not one of us lives for himself,*
> *and not one dies for himself;*
> *for if we live, we live for the Lord,*
> *or if we die, we die for the Lord;*

therefore whether we live or die,

we are the Lord's.

∞ Romans 14:7–8 NASB, emphasis added

Romans 14:8 is a reminder of who we are and what our life is all about. Our preeminent loyalty is to God because we *belong to Him.*

Have you ever heard God described as a jealous God? Actually, that is God's description of Himself. The idea of a jealous God was unpalatable to me until I uncovered the sweetness in this virtue. The source of His jealousy is His uncompromising love for us. He desires our greatest good, our highest attainment. His hopes and plans for us include abundant joy and peace, satisfaction and contentment. He envisions holiness, righteousness, and completeness for us as we are transformed into His image. Because He loves us so very much, He is protectively and possessively jealous of *anything* or *anyone* that will rob us of the ultimate best He has for us. That is why His first commandment is "You shall have no other gods before me" (Exodus 20:3). God knows that other gods in our lives, whether they be materialistic or spiritual, or just plain self-centeredness, will lure our hearts away from Him and diminish our capacity to be all He wants for us.

The outcome of our lives is of utmost importance to Him. He doesn't want us settling for less than the best. Therefore, God jealously guards what belongs to Him—and we belong to Him. Our devotion and time belong to Him. Our affections belong to Him. We are His. He bought us with a price, and you'd better believe He's protecting His investment.

Because God is committed to our transformation, He will see to it that the work He began in us will be brought to its glorious conclusion. His persistent love won't let us wander too far. He will go to the ends of the earth to bring us back, and He will discipline us when He has to, because He is jealous for our good. He wants us to keep moving forward. He doesn't want us to stay where we are.

Eleven years ago, I was living a comfortable Christian life in Dallas, surrounded by friends, a good church, Christian radio, and a ministry I was involved in. I didn't realize what was happening to me, but God was aware of my spiritual stagnation, and He loved me too much to leave me there. I can now see His providential hand moving me from Texas to Mississippi, not allowing me to stay where I was, lapsing into mediocrity. There was too much at stake: two preschool-age children whose lives were in my hands and whose spiritual development depended on mine; a husband, my partner for life, whom I could potentially harm or help; and any hope for having a significant ministry in the lives of others.

Although I sincerely desired to grow in my faith and attempted to fit in Bible study and prayer, I was limited by the exhaustion of motherhood, having no energy left for such pursuits. Consequently, my spiritual life was characterized by distraction, guilt, and weariness. In a theoretical sense, I understood the connection between knowing God's Word and having a vibrant, thriving relationship with God, but my distractions kept me from devoting the time I should. Struggling with guilt over not making God a priority, I continued to grow weary of attempting but failing to be consistent in Bible study. Each missed opportunity moved me closer to giving up completely. I was tempted to put aside my own spiritual well-being until my family was grown, but then where would I get the wisdom and courage I needed to raise up a godly heritage? The frustration was mounting, but there seemed to be no workable solution.

In my case, something drastic was called for. God had to yank me out of my secure place and send me four hundred miles away, with no friends, no Christian radio, and no ministry. He stripped away the things I had become dependent on so that I would become dependent on Him.

That day in Chattanooga when I heard the book of Colossians quoted, I saw my impoverished condition. Although I was a sincere and dedicated Christian, the truth was that I didn't know God's Word. I had reached a plateau and had been stuck there for some time. I knew enough to get by, to "talk the talk," but there was no real depth in it. No wonder I wasn't growing and changing. I was neglecting the very thing God had intended to use to transform me.

With every ounce of determination in me, I resolved to make a change. As a busy mom, with a never-ending list of things to accomplish in a day's time, I didn't have any extra hours in my day, but I found extra *minutes* and extra *moments* when I could include God's Word. I added Scripture memory to my morning routine, using the time when my hands were occupied but my mind was free. I used driving time and waiting time. I traded moments of daydreaming for moments of meditation.

Over the next few months and years, the transforming power of God's Word began to alter my thinking and my attitudes, slowly building convictions that became the foundation for my future. I've heard my pastor say this about the difference between an opinion and a conviction: "An opinion is something *you hold;* a conviction is something that *holds you.*" When I tell others that God has given us everything we need for life and godliness through our knowledge of Him, this is not merely my opinion; it is a solid conviction. This conviction holds me firmly and shapes my role as a wife and a mother, a citizen of my country, and a child of God. Years ago I would have told you that the Bible was essential for a healthy, dynamic relationship with God, but that was only my opinion. Now I can tell you with unwavering conviction.

Convictions lead us to decide what we will do with our lives, how we will invest our time, which activities will get our attention. For example, my convictions about God's Word began to transform my desire to study the Bible. I reached the point where it wasn't enough just to know the words of 2 Timothy; I wanted to know what they meant, and that could only come from studying. Memorizing Scripture gave me the motivation to study at a more in-depth level. It gave me a hunger to understand what was written. Studying opened up so much more than I could ever get from just memorizing. The disciplines of memorizing and studying have worked in tandem in my life so that I could know the heart of the passage, not just know the passage by heart.

Up to that point in my Christian life, I had never made studying the Bible a priority. I went to Bible studies and even taught Bible studies myself. But I didn't feel the need for intense Bible study. My philosophy was, "Let the experts study, and they can give us the highlights." My days were occupied in serving God and my family, and quite frankly, I wasn't convinced that the extra effort required would be worth it. And, besides,

I was pretty confident that I knew as much about the Bible as most Christians.

Although that may have been true, it only contributed to my apathy. I was comfortable fitting in with the majority. I measured myself by others and thought I was doing pretty well, considering I didn't grow up in church and had learned everything as an adult. But memorizing Scripture day in, day out showed me that my standard should not be what everyone else was doing. My standard should be determined by God. I didn't experience an internal struggle to give studying the Bible a bigger time slot in my day. I was *compelled* toward it. I was *driven;* I was *thirsty* for Bible study. I was in a hurry to make up for lost time. I had such an insatiable desire to know God's Word that I was willing to do anything to achieve that.

Studying moved up the ranks on my priority list, not out of dutiful acquiescence, but because nothing else seemed as important. I let other projects and involvements go, most of which I can't even remember because I don't miss them. I am no longer dependent on the highlights shared by someone else who is a student of the Word. As I give time to independent study, God shows me truth that stimulates my own thinking, leading to a greater probability of remembering what I have learned.

Memorizing was not an end in itself. It was a stepping-stone to a more comprehensive approach to the Bible. I read it more; I studied it more; I listened more intently when it was preached. I felt as though I had a greater stake in what was written there because I had made it my own. It was God's message to *me,* and I had never fully grasped that before.

Our family has been so blessed to have dear and

precious friends who are missionaries all over the world. Having followed many of their lives, we have observed common threads in their ministries. Some of our friends are working in France, and their experience is typical.

First, because they desired to have a dynamic, long-term ministry in France, they had to learn the native language. They would not be effective in the new setting without it.

Second, taking a once-a-week French class while they lived in the United States wasn't sufficient preparation for having a ministry to French-speaking people living in France.

Third, it wasn't enough for them just to learn to speak the correct words. They needed to understand the culture, the people, and the history that affected the thinking and attitudes behind the words.

So the most common training for missionaries is a total immersion in the culture and the language, a daily bombardment of faces, ideas, thoughts, customs, and lifestyle. The process moves from learning to *speak* in French to actually *thinking* in French. Without that transition, their ministry would not have moved beyond the infant stage.

There is a parallel here in Scripture memory, and we need to be careful to understand it, or we will lose sight of the real purpose before us. It's not enough just to know the words of the Bible; rather, we need to be so immersed in God's Word that we will think biblically. In every situation I face, I want to view it through the filter of God's Word. I want to think God's thoughts. I want to dream God's dreams. I want to know His way. To have the exact words stored in my brain is a valuable asset, but it will never be enough. If I go no deeper than just "the words," it will be a waste of time, an exercise in futility.

My goal, instead, is nothing short of a total transformation of my thinking, which in turn will bring about an alteration of my being. I want to be speaking God's language, not merely reciting His words but communicating His intentions and expressing His heart. As in learning a second language, this is not possible through a once-a-week exposure to God's Word. Without total immersion into God's Word, we will not be thinking or living biblically.

This is what Scripture memory has done for me. By adding a new verse almost every day, and constantly reviewing other passages throughout my day, I have found the means to meditate day and night on God's Word. As I mentioned earlier, the change that has taken place in my life has come from the process, not the achievement. My mind has been trained to turn to God's Word many times throughout the day. Before I began to memorize, I was *exposed* to Scripture, but I was not *immersed* in Scripture. Now I truly see the difference.

God's Word was intended to be a transforming agent in our lives. As we spend time immersed in the Scriptures, it is constantly working in us. Paul wrote to the Thessalonians, "When you received the word of God, which you heard from us, you accepted it not as the word of men, but as it actually is, the word of God, *which is at work in you who believe*" (1 Thessalonians 2:13, emphasis added).

That is why Moses instructed the Israelites to talk about God's Law day and night, when they rose and when they lay down, when they went out and when they came in. God knew that focusing on His Word throughout the day would keep them on the right path, not veering too far to the right or to the left. This obedience would keep them exactly where God wanted them to be, in continual communion with Him and transforming their nation into a people for God's glory.

God wants you and me to mature and be transformed; He's committed to it. He gave us His Spirit and His Word for this purpose. Scripture tells us to "be transformed by the renewing of your mind" (Romans 12:2). The word *renew* can mean to make fresh again. Am I implying that God's Word becomes stale and old? No, it's our minds that become stale and depleted. For example, we often ignore familiar truths, giving them a yawn instead of our attention, assuming there is "nothing new" in them. We rob ourselves of treasures when we forget that God's Word is living and active. It is not merely a Book of history but is alive and working even today.

Such was the case for me with the Christmas story. Through the years, hearing it told over and over, I had lost the wonder of it. A year ago, a church asked me if I would come and recite the Christmas story from Luke. I had to say no because I didn't know it. Thinking it wouldn't take me very long to memorize, I put it on my list of passages to memorize for the next year. When the time came to work on it, I got a fresh spiral and was about to write out the verses.

Typically, the story is told beginning with the words "In the sixth month, God sent the angel Gabriel to Nazareth" (Luke 1:26). I looked back a few verses to find out, "In the sixth month" of what? In the sixth month of Elizabeth's pregnancy. Oh, yes, Elizabeth; did we forget her? And what about Zechariah? Isn't he part of the story? I decided to start again at the real beginning, Luke 1:1.

I have spent the last several months on the first two chapters of Luke, and it has brought about a renewal of my attitude. I was reminded that Christ's birth was not a last-ditch effort by God to save the world from the mess people had gotten themselves into. It was a plan designed before the foundation of the world, unfolded for us through the pages of history, revealed in the fullness of time. The birth of Jesus was the fulfillment of a promise made to Abraham centuries before but never forgotten by God. Taking the time to meditate on this story one verse at a time made it new again.

Have *you* lost the wonder of the Christmas story, or other stories in the Bible? Well, now you know that the problem is not with the story, but with you. Your mind needs to be refreshed and renewed. This is a first step in the transformation process. The psalmist wrote, "I will never forget your precepts, for by them you have preserved my life" (Psalm 119:93).

One of the things I have come to appreciate about God is His practicality. Because He wants us to know truth and to have direction for life, He has made that available to us. God isn't sending us on a wild-goose chase searching for answers to the issues of life. They're right here in His Word—everything we need for life and godliness. Moses told Israel,

> *Now what I am commanding you today is not too difficult for you or beyond your reach. It is not up in heaven, so that you have to ask, "Who will ascend into heaven to get it and proclaim it to us so we may obey it?" Nor is it beyond the sea, so that you have to ask, "Who will cross the sea to get it and proclaim it to us so we may obey it?" No, the word is very near you; it is in your mouth and in your heart so you may obey it.*

∽ Deuteronomy 30:11–14

God's ways are not too difficult to understand. Nor

did God put them out of reach so that we have to wait for heaven to find out what He wants for us. God gave us His Word to be in our hearts and on our lips so that we might live an obedient life, one that is pleasing to Him.

I don't know why God allowed me into His family, why He drew me close and revealed Himself to me. But every glimpse of His mercy toward me stirs a longing in my heart to live worthy of that calling and that sacrifice. How can I live such a life? It's utterly impossible on my own. I am keenly aware of my limitations, now more than ever. I have no innate ability to distinguish between God's unadulterated truth and the world's skillfully disguised half-truths. I don't have the courage or the strength to deal with life's complexities and the seemingly insurmountable challenges I will face in this life. Thankfully, I am not attempting this on my own. I've found the source of my enabling. It is not *exposure* to God's Word but *immersion* in God's Word. God's Spirit and God's Word, both living in me, will be sufficient for today and tomorrow and next week.

Isn't this what Jesus was referring to in His discourse about the vine and the branches? It is not enough for the branch to be near the vine, to be exposed to the vine; it has to be *connected* to the vine and constantly drawing its nourishment from the vine. Jesus told His disciples to abide in Him, to stay connected to Him, so that their lives would bear fruit and bring glory to His Father. Jesus said, "Abide in Me, and I in you. As the branch cannot bear fruit of itself unless it abides in the vine, so neither can you unless you abide in Me" (John 15:4 NASB).

But there are more consequences than just being powerless, fruitless, and useless, devastating as those might be. Fruit bearing is not an end in itself. Jesus said,

"If you keep My commandments you will *abide in My love;* just as I have kept My Father's commandments and *abide in His love.* These things I have spoken to you, that *My joy may be in you,* and that your joy may be made full" (John 15:10–11 NASB, emphasis added). Jesus is talking about love and joy. After all, what would be the point of great fruitfulness to God if there were no love or joy? The fruit of abiding in Christ is *obedience,* which is our gateway to deeper intimacy with Christ. If true communion is a mutual sharing, an identifying with another, then when we obey God we identify with Christ's obedience to His Father and we share in the joy He experienced when He obeyed.

Yes, we want fruitfulness; we want power for accomplishing God's will in our lives; we want usefulness in God's kingdom. But our hearts want more and will not be satisfied with anything less than sharing in the love and joy of Christ. This is what we were created for—a meaningful relationship with God. For me, that's what memorizing Scripture is all about!

When I think about why I have continued memorizing and reviewing God's Word, rarely ever missing a day, the answer is simple. Memorizing Scripture has brought vitality to my daily walk with God. Basking in the warmth of His presence, I am the recipient of an endless supply of His goodness. God is my sustenance, and His Word revealed that to me. God is the balm for my wounds, and His Word brings the healing. God is my antidote for weariness, and His Word gives me the reasons to persevere. God is my safe place when life disappoints me, and His Word is where I run for comfort. God is my heart's deepest joy that no earthly pleasure can duplicate. His Word living in me made that a reality. I have taken hold of God's Word, and God's Word has taken hold of me. It is more than words written on 3 x 5 cards; it is words written on my heart!

Appendix

LONG-TERM
SUGGESTIONS

$\mathcal{N}$ow that I have been memorizing for over ten years, I have some recommendations for those who want to take Scripture memory seriously, specifically in the area of what to memorize and how to review. Some of these tips I learned accidentally; others I purposely researched.

WHAT TO MEMORIZE

∽ *Choose a variety of topics and authors to give you a wide spectrum of knowledge.* By memorizing passages from different authors, you will get distinct, though complementary, perspectives and insights unique to each author. Notice, for example, the different authors in these passages and books:

Sermon on the Mount—Jesus
Philippians—Paul
1 Peter—Peter
James—James
Luke 1–2—Luke
Hebrews—author unknown
Isaiah 55—Isaiah
Psalm 62—David

∞ *Choose passages that mean something special to you, not necessarily what everyone else is doing.* You will be more motivated if you already feel a personal connection. For example, I memorized 1 Peter during a time of suffering and trials. I held on to each word for my daily survival.

∞ *Before you begin a memorization project, count the number of verses, and project how long the task will take you to accomplish.* Look also at how long the chapters are, because you may want to plan on a chapter a month, unless it is more than five chapters. For a longer book, take a break somewhere in the middle just for review before moving on. This is like counting the cost before you jump into something you may not have the endurance to finish. Ask yourself if you are up for the challenge of a long book, or if you would rather do a short passage. For example, here is a sample list, starting with shorter passages and ending with longer passages.

Psalm 8—9 verses
1 Corinthians 13—13 verses
Psalm 145—21 verses
Jude—25 verses
Proverbs 31—31 verses
Titus—46 verses

2 Peter—61 verses
Acts 6:8–7:60 (Stephen's defense)—68 verses
2 Timothy—83 verses
Colossians—95 verses
1 John—105 verses
Matthew 5–7 (Sermon on the Mount)—111 verses
Luke 1:1–2:40 (Christmas story)—120 verses
Galatians—149 verses
2 Corinthians—257 verses
Hebrews—303 verses
Revelation—404 verses

WHAT NOT TO MEMORIZE

This is just a word of caution, so as to avoid frustration when you have already begun a project. Some books or passages are so similar to others that it can be confusing to try to memorize both. Colossians and Ephesians have many verses that are almost identical, and it would require immense concentration to memorize both of these. I would do one or the other. Jude and 2 Peter also have repeated themes.

Another confusion comes with the greetings and closings of Paul's letters. They are all similar, with only slight differences. I often get mixed up even now. If I had it to do again, I would learn some other passages in between Paul's letters, so that I had one book firmly established before I tackled something similar. Read over what you would like to memorize before you begin so that you can recognize trouble spots and perhaps change your plan.

Some of the psalms have exact repeated phrases. The danger here is that you may begin reciting one and end up in the other. Many New Testament books also quote Old Testament references, such as Hebrews, which quotes the Law, the Psalms, and the Prophets. Just try to avoid duplicating verses in different books.

HOW TO REVIEW

You probably remember my suggestion to pick a certain day of the week for each book or passage. Here are some examples:

Sunday—2 Timothy
Monday—Philippians
Tuesday—Sermon on the Mount
Wednesday—1 Peter
Thursday—Ephesians
Friday—1 Thessalonians
Saturday—(all) Psalms

But what do you do when you have more than seven passages to review? If you start to double up, putting two passages on each day, you can become too accomplishment oriented and lose track of your real purpose, which is to know God and walk closely with Him. I know, because this has happened to me.

I have a system that works for me because it's methodical but flexible. I have a dated chart listing all my passages in chronological order, or the order in which they appear in the Bible. Starting at the top, I review that passage for two days in a row, each day putting half an X on my chart. This is just for personal accountability—no other reason. The following two days I move on to the next passage, and so on until the list is completed.

The reason I spend two days instead of just one is

that I found that the first day I am usually concentrating so much on getting the text exactly correct that I can miss what God is saying. The second day is more relaxed, and I am freer to meditate on the truth presented. With several short psalms, I may do two or three together on the same day.

When I finish my list, I go back up to the top, put in a new date, and start over. The date lets me know how diligent or how slack I have been. For example, if I have twelve passages to review and it took me more than two months, then I know I have either been lazy or possibly have taken more time on some passages. This schedule gives me some freedom without being legalistic and yet still keeps me on track.

You can break down very long books into sections if you know you can't cover the entire book in one day. For example, Hebrews, which takes about forty-five minutes to review, can be divided into chapters 1–4; 5–8; 9–10; and 11–13. On any given day, do as much as you can and then pick it up the next day where you left off. Ideally, do it all at one time if you can, so that you don't interrupt the teaching. But that's not always possible. When I am alone, I use long car trips for longer passages since it makes the time go by more quickly, and I then arrive at my destination revived and rejuvenated. I realize this may not work for some of you, for mothers of preschoolers rarely get to go anywhere alone.

When I memorized the book of Revelation, it took me two and a half years to finish. I then spent two more years reviewing the entire book every week. Because I could not fit in seventy-five minutes at one time, I divided the book into seven-day segments. My daily routine included a three-mile walk, using ten to fifteen minutes of that time for reviewing my Revelation chapters. This helped me to get the text solidified in my mind, and now I only review it periodically as part of my review chart.

Experiment; try different ways and see what works for you. For women, our lifestyles seem to change every few years, so we need to keep adapting our methods. The main thing is to keep going. Don't quit; keep God's Word in your heart and mind throughout your day, whatever else your day may hold.

NOTES

Chapter Two
My Goal: Like a Tree Planted by Streams of Water

1. Spiros Zodhiates, *The Complete Word Study: Old Testament,* gen. ed, Warren Baker (Chattanooga, Tenn.: AMG, 1994), entry no. 1897, page 2310.

2. Henry George Liddell and Robert Scott, comp., *A Greek-English Lexicon,* 9th ed., revised by Henry Stuart Jones; with a supplement (Oxford: Clarendon Press, 1968), 1096.

3. G. B. Funderburk, in *The Zondervan Pictorial Encyclopedia of the Bible,* ed. Merrill C. Tenney and Stephen Barabas (Grand Rapids: Zondervan, 1976), 4:163.

Chapter Six
Benefit #2: To Obey Is Better than Sacrifice

1. James Strong, "A Concise Dictionary of the Words in the Hebrew Bible," in *The Exaustive Concordance of the Bible* (Nashville: Abingdon), entry no. 6743.

2. Spiros Zodhiates, *The Complete Word Study: Old Testament*, gen. ed, Warren Baker (Chattanooga, Tenn.: AMG, 1994), entry no. 7919, page 2373.

3. Spiros Zodhiates, *The Complete Word Study Dictionary: New Testament*, rev. ed. (Chattanooga, Tenn.: AMG, 1993), entry no. 1718, page 578.

4. Ibid., entry no. 3438, page 995.

Janet Pope has a speaking ministry that includes
women's conferences and retreats,
church services and events,
evangelistic outreaches and other gatherings.

You may contact Janet at:
Foundations For Living
P. O. Box 15356
Hattiesburg, MS 39404

(601) 582-2000; (601) 582-8100 (fax)
e-mail: janet@foundationsforliving.org